INTRODUCING
ISSUES WITH
OPPOSING
VIEWPOINTS®

Gun Control

Noël Merino, *Book Editor*

GREENHAVEN PRESS
A part of Gale, Cengage Learning

GALE
CENGAGE Learning·

Detroit • New York • San Francisco • New Haven, Conn • Waterville, Maine • London

Elizabeth Des Chenes, *Director, Publishing Solutions*

For more information, contact:
Greenhaven Press
27500 Drake Rd.
Farmington Hills, MI 48331-3535
Or you can visit our Internet site at gale.cengage.com

For product information and technology assistance, contact us at

Gale Customer Support, 1-800-877-4253
For permission to use material from this text or product, submit all requests online at www.cengage.com/permissions

Further permissions questions can be e-mailed to permissionrequest@cengage.com

Articles in Greenhaven Press anthologies are often edited for length to meet page requirements. In addition, original titles of these works are changed to clearly present the main thesis and to explicitly indicate the author's opinion. Every effort is made to ensure that Greenhaven Press accurately reflects the original intent of the authors. Every effort has been made to trace the owners of copyrighted material.

Cover image © koi88/Shutterstock.com.

LIBRARY OF CONGRESS CATALOGING-IN-PUBLICATION DATA

Gun control / Noël Merino, book editor.
    p. cm. -- (Introducing issues with opposing viewpoints)
  Includes bibliographical references and index.
  ISBN 978-0-7377-6278-5 (hbk.)
  1. Gun control--United States. I. Merino, Noël.
  HV7436.G86343 2012
  363.330973--dc23

                                                  2012022604

Printed in the United States of America
1 2 3 4 5 6 7 16 15 14 13 12

Contents

Chapter 3: What Measures Should Be Taken to Reduce Gun Violence?

Foreword

Indulging in a wide spectrum of ideas, beliefs, and perspectives is a critical cornerstone of democracy. After all, it is often debates over differences of opinion, such as whether to legalize abortion, how to treat prisoners, or when to enact the death penalty, that shape our society and drive it forward. Such diversity of thought is frequently regarded as the hallmark of a healthy and civilized culture. As the Reverend Clifford Schutjer of the First Congregational Church in Mansfield, Ohio, declared in a 2001 sermon, "Surrounding oneself with only like-minded people, restricting what we listen to or read only to what we find agreeable is irresponsible. Refusing to entertain doubts once we make up our minds is a subtle but deadly form of arrogance." With this advice in mind, Introducing Issues with Opposing Viewpoints books aim to open readers' minds to the critically divergent views that comprise our world's most important debates.

Introducing Issues with Opposing Viewpoints simplifies for students the enormous and often overwhelming mass of material now available via print and electronic media. Collected in every volume is an array of opinions that captures the essence of a particular controversy or topic. Introducing Issues with Opposing Viewpoints books embody the spirit of nineteenth-century journalist Charles A. Dana's axiom: "Fight for your opinions, but do not believe that they contain the whole truth, or the only truth." Absorbing such contrasting opinions teaches students to analyze the strength of an argument and compare it to its opposition. From this process readers can inform and strengthen their own opinions, or be exposed to new information that will change their minds. Introducing Issues with Opposing Viewpoints is a mosaic of different voices. The authors are statesmen, pundits, academics, journalists, corporations, and ordinary people who have felt compelled to share their experiences and ideas in a public forum. Their words have been collected from newspapers, journals, books, speeches, interviews, and the Internet, the fastest growing body of opinionated material in the world.

Introducing Issues with Opposing Viewpoints shares many of the well-known features of its critically acclaimed parent series, Opposing Viewpoints. The articles are presented in a pro/con format, allowing readers to absorb divergent perspectives side by side. Active reading questions preface each viewpoint, requiring the student to approach the material thoughtfully and carefully. Useful charts, graphs, and cartoons supplement each article. A thorough introduction provides readers with crucial background on an issue. An annotated bibliography points the reader toward articles, books, and websites that contain additional information on the topic. An appendix of organizations to contact contains a wide variety of charities, nonprofit organizations, political groups, and private enterprises that each hold a position on the issue at hand. Finally, a comprehensive index allows readers to locate content quickly and efficiently.

Introducing Issues with Opposing Viewpoints is also significantly different from Opposing Viewpoints. As the series title implies, its presentation will help introduce students to the concept of opposing viewpoints and learn to use this material to aid in critical writing and debate. The series' four-color, accessible format makes the books attractive and inviting to readers of all levels. In addition, each viewpoint has been carefully edited to maximize a reader's understanding of the content. Short but thorough viewpoints capture the essence of an argument. A substantial, thought-provoking essay question placed at the end of each viewpoint asks the student to further investigate the issues raised in the viewpoint, compare and contrast two authors' arguments, or consider how one might go about forming an opinion on the topic at hand. Each viewpoint contains sidebars that include at-a-glance information and handy statistics. A Facts About section located in the back of the book further supplies students with relevant facts and figures.

Following in the tradition of the Opposing Viewpoints series, Greenhaven Press continues to provide readers with invaluable exposure to the controversial issues that shape our world. As John Stuart Mill once wrote: "The only way in which a human being can make some approach to knowing the whole of a subject is by hearing what can be said about it by persons of every variety of opinion and studying all modes in which it can be looked at by every character of mind. No wise man ever acquired his wisdom in any mode but this." It is to this principle that Introducing Issues with Opposing Viewpoints books are dedicated.

Introduction

"All of us have to do some soul searching to figure out: How does something like this happen? And that means that we examine the laws and the context for what happened, as well as the specifics of the incident."

—President Barack Obama, speech on March 23, 2012,
regarding the Trayvon Martin shooting

On February 26, 2012, seventeen-year-old Trayvon Martin was shot and killed by twenty-eight-year-old community watch coordinator George Zimmerman. Martin was walking to his father's fiancée's home in a gated community in Sanford, Florida, when Zimmerman saw him. Zimmerman called 9-1-1 to report what he described as suspicious behavior on the part of Martin. Police later arrived at the scene to find an unarmed Martin dead from being shot by Zimmerman; Zimmerman claims he shot Martin in self-defense. Zimmerman was not arrested right away because of Florida's stand-your-ground law, which allows a person to use deadly force if he or she feels threatened by bodily harm. Zimmerman was charged with second-degree murder by the state attorney on April 11, 2012, and Zimmerman turned himself in. What will become of this case remains to be seen, but what is certain is that the case stirred much controversy about Florida's stand-your-ground law and similar laws in other states.

Florida was the first state to pass such a law, which was enacted in April 2005. Such laws are an extension of the so-called castle doctrine, which permits the use of deadly force for self-defense of one's home. This tradition of castle doctrine in American law, however, has typically required that a person who uses deadly force during a home invasion or attack prove that such force was reasonable. Stand-your-ground laws expand this doctrine in three ways: First, the laws eliminate a duty to retreat when one is threatened in one's home, allowing one to "stand one's ground." Second, the laws shift the burden of proof: Rather than requiring a defendant who injures or kills another to prove that he or she acted in self-defense, the law shifts the burden of proof to the prosecutor, requiring that the victim prove "beyond a reasonable doubt" that the defendant *did not* act in self-defense. Finally, many of the laws expand the realm where deadly force can be used in self-defense from one's home to one's vehicle, workplace, and—in many states—to public places, as in the case of the Florida law.

At the time of the Martin shooting, twenty-four more states had joined Florida in passing stand-your-ground laws that allow the use of deadly force in self-defense without an obligation to retreat first: Alabama, Arizona, Georgia, Idaho, Illinois, Indiana, Kansas, Kentucky, Louisiana, Michigan, Mississippi, Montana, Nevada, New Hampshire, North Carolina, Oklahoma, Oregon, South Carolina, South Dakota, Tennessee, Texas, Utah, Washington, and West Virginia. Five other states—Alaska, Iowa, Massachusetts, Nebraska, and New York—had such laws under consideration.

Reaction to stand-your-ground laws has been extremely divided. The National Rifle Association (NRA) has been a leading proponent of the laws, helping to get them passed. NRA lobbyist Marion Hammer warns about rushing to judgment about stand-your-ground laws based on one case: "This law is not about one incident. It's about protecting the right of law-abiding people to protect themselves when they are attacked. There is absolutely nothing wrong with the law."[1] John R. Lott Jr., author of *More Guns, Less Crime*, says that stand-your-ground laws protect victims from having to retreat when to do so is not in their best interest: "Forcing a victim to take time to retreat can put their life in jeopardy, and a prosecutor might argue that a victim didn't retreat sufficiently." Furthermore, Lott says that "allowing victims to defend themselves not only protects the lives of victims who come under attack, but deters criminals from attacking to begin with."[2] By shifting the burden of proof from victims to attackers, the idea is that criminal activity will be prevented.

The Brady Campaign to Prevent Gun Violence has fought against such laws, calling them "shoot first, ask questions later" laws. Opponents of stand-your-ground laws worry that the laws shift the enforcement of law and responsibility for public safety from law enforcement officials to vigilante citizens. Mark Glaze, the director of Mayors Against Illegal Guns, says, "It's not about standing your ground, it's about taking authority away from police and ignoring

400 years of common law that has always allowed you to defend your-self."[3] There is also a worry about what such laws say about the value of human life. Former federal prosecutor and current law professor Joëlle Anne Moreno says that one worry about stand-your-ground laws is that they "change how we view the sanctity of human life. If we're allowed to shoot somebody for reaching into your car to grab a purse, does it mean that we don't value human life the way we thought we did?"[4]

Many hope that the shooting of Martin leads to the elimination of stand-your-ground laws. Adam S. Cohen, who teaches at Yale Law School, opines, "There is no way to undo what happened in the Zimmerman-Martin encounter, but some good can still come of it: it could lead states to repeal their misguided 'stand your ground' laws."[5] Others argue that the killing of Martin is not actually covered by Florida's stand-your-ground law and so does not implicate the law in any way: "There is no connection between Florida's Stand Your Ground law and the killing of Trayvon Martin. Martin did not break into Zimmerman's home. Zimmerman was not under attack when he initially encountered Martin."[6] Whatever the outcome, the controversy over the case reflects the polarized views about gun control in America. There is great debate in America about the meaning of the Second Amendment, the efficacy of gun control legislation, and the need for greater regulation, as is clear by the variety of positions taken by the authors of the viewpoints in *Introducing Issues with Opposing Viewpoints: Gun Control.*

Notes

1. Quoted in Dara Kam, "'Stand Your Ground' Self-Defense Gun Law Draws Protests—and Governor Advises New Look at It," *Palm Beach (FL) Post*, March 20, 2012. www.palmbeachpost.com /news/news/state-regional/stand-your-ground-self-defense-gun -law-draws-pro-1/nLhpY.
2. John R. Lott Jr., "It's Not About Stand Your Ground," *National Review Online*, March 28, 2012. www.nationalreview.com/articles /294609/it-s-not-about-stand-your-ground-john-r-lott-jr.
3. Quoted in E.J. Dionne Jr., "Why the NRA Pushes 'Stand Your Ground,'" *Washington Post*, April 15, 2012. www.wash

ingtonpost.com/opinions/why-the-nra-pushes-stand-your
-ground/2012/04/15/gIQAL458JT_story.html.

4. Quoted in Patrik Jonsson, "Trayvon Martin Case Reveals Confusion over How Stand Your Ground Works," *Christian Science Monitor*, April 11, 2012. www.csmonitor.com/USA/Justice/2012/0411 /Trayvon-Martin-case-reveals-confusion-over-how-Stand-Your -Ground-works.

5. Adam Cohen, "The Growing Movement to Repeal 'Stand Your Ground' Laws," *Time*, April 16, 2012. http://ideas.time.com /2012/04/16/the-growing-movement-to-repeal-stand-your -ground-laws.

6. Quoted in Tim Lynch, "Stand Your Ground Not Responsible for Trayvon Martin's Death," *Jurist*, April 6, 2012. http://jurist.org /hotline/2012/04/tim-lynch-trayvon-martin.php.

Chapter 1

Should People Have the Right to Have Guns?

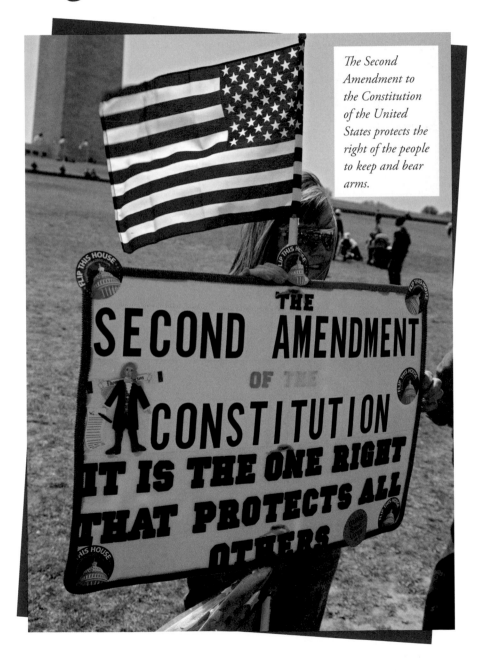

The Second Amendment to the Constitution of the United States protects the right of the people to keep and bear arms.

Viewpoint

1

The Second Amendment Protects the Right to Keep and Bear Arms

Robert A. Levy

"Apparently embarrassed by seven decades without a coherent explanation of the right celebrated during the framing era as 'the true palladium of liberty', the court rediscovered the Second Amendment."

In the following viewpoint Robert A. Levy argues that a 2008 US Supreme Court decision makes clear that the Second Amendment protects the right of individuals to have guns. Levy claims that the court rightfully determined that the right "to keep and bear arms" is not limited to the military and that the government may not ban guns. Levy claims that the court's decision reflects the original meaning of the Second Amendment.

Levy is chairman of the board of directors at the DC-based libertarian think tank the Cato Institute and coauthor of *The Dirty Dozen: How Twelve Supreme Court Cases Radically Expanded Government and Eroded Freedom.*

AS YOU READ, CONSIDER THE FOLLOWING QUESTIONS:
  1. According to the author, in what year did the District of Columbia ban residents from owning handguns?
  2. Levy claims that the US Supreme Court's majority decision in *District of Columbia v. Heller* (2008) was held by how many of the nine justices?
  3. According to Levy, how many state legislatures have rejected bans on private handgun ownership?

"The right of the people to keep and bear Arms shall not be infringed." That's the operative clause of the Second Amendment nearly erased from the Constitution in 1939 by a muddled and confusing Supreme Court opinion in *United States v. Miller.*

Last week [June 26, 2008], apparently embarrassed by seven decades without a coherent explanation of the right celebrated during the framing era as "the true palladium of liberty," the court rediscovered the Second Amendment. More than five years after six Washington residents challenged the city's 32-year-old ban on all functional firearms in the home, the court held in *District of Columbia v. Heller* that the gun ban is unconstitutional.

The Arguments for a Ban

Indeed it is. For starters, no handgun could be registered in D.C. [District of Columbia]. Even pistols registered prior to the 1976 ban could not be carried from room to room in the home without a license, which was unobtainable. Moreover, all firearms in the home, including rifles and shotguns, had to be unloaded and either disassembled or bound by a trigger lock. In effect, no one in the district could possess a functional firearm in his or her own residence. And the law applied not just to "unfit" persons such as felons, minors or the mentally incompetent, but across the board to ordinary, honest, responsible citizens.

D.C. Mayor Adrian M. Fenty raised two principal arguments in support of the city's ban.

First, the Second Amendment ensures only that members of state militias are properly armed, not that private citizens can have guns for self-defense and other personal uses.

Second, even if the Second Amendment protects private ownership of firearms for non-militia purposes, D.C.'s legislature can constitutionally ban all handguns if it determines, for example, that rifles and shotguns in the home are a reasonable alternative means of self-defense. The court rejected both arguments.

The Supreme Court's Decision

Essentially, wrote Justice Antonin Scalia for a 5–4 majority, the militia clause announces one purpose of the Second Amendment, but does not limit or expand the right to keep and bear arms expressly stated in the operative clause. Nor does the court's prior precedent *United States v. Miller* say otherwise. It establishes simply that some weapons [for example], a sawed-off shotgun are not protected unless they can be shown to have military utility and be in common use.

Moreover, declared Scalia, the District may not categorically ban "an entire class of 'arms' that Americans overwhelmingly choose for the lawful purpose of self-defense." Alternative weapons, such as long guns, have numerous disadvantages and must, under a provision of D.C. law, be kept unloaded and either disassembled or trigger-locked. That provision does not contain an exception for self-defense.

FAST FACT

The full text of the Second Amendment says: "A well regulated militia being necessary to the security of a free state, the right of the people to keep and bear arms shall not be infringed."

In his dissenting opinion, Justice John Paul Stevens not only quarreled with Scalia's interpretation of historical events, but he also implied that Scalia had abandoned true judicial conservatism by dragging the court into the "political thicket" of gun control. "Judicial restraint would be far wiser," wrote Stevens, than mediating a political process that is "working exactly as it should."

In the Supreme Court's decision in United States v. Miller, *Justice Antonin Scalia (pictured) wrote for the majority that the militia clause in the Second Amendment announces the amendment's purpose but that it neither limits nor expands the right to keep and bear arms.*

The Issue of State Gun Laws

Justice Stephen Breyer, also dissenting in *Heller*, proffered this extraordinary statement: "The decision threatens to throw into doubt the constitutionality of gun laws throughout the United States." Nonsense. Forty-four states have constitutional provisions protecting an individual right to keep and bear arms.

States with Constitutional Provisions Stating the Right to Keep and Bear Arms

States in which residents can legally keep and bear arms

Taken from: Eugene Volokh, "State Constitutional Rights to Keep and Bear Arms," *Texas Review of Law and Politics*, vol. 11, no. 1, 2006.

Legislatures in all 50 states have rejected bans on private handgun ownership. Concealed carry is permitted, with varying degrees of administrative discretion, in all states except Wisconsin and Illinois. Those laws would have remained on the books no matter what the Supreme Court had decided in *Heller*. The major impact of the court's opinion will be felt, not "throughout the United States," but in the cities and other political subdivisions that have enacted draconian gun laws under delegated power from state governments.

Heller is merely the opening salvo in a series of litigations that will ultimately resolve what weapons and persons can be regulated and what restrictions are permissible. Near term, the court will also have to decide whether Second Amendment rights can be enforced against state and local governments [the Supreme Court ruled that they could be in *McDonald v. Chicago* (2010)]. Despite those remaining hurdles, it's fair to say that the court's blockbuster decision makes the prospects for reviving the original meaning of the Second Amendment substantially brighter. And given the unfolding presidential contest, it's also fair to say that the court's razor-thin majority conveys a crucial message: Judicial nominations matter.

EVALUATING THE AUTHOR'S ARGUMENTS:

In this viewpoint Robert A. Levy claims that the original intent of the Second Amendment was for individuals to be able to own guns. Which other authors in this chapter agree with Levy on this point? Which disagree?

The Second Amendment Does Not Guarantee Gun Rights Without Regulation

"The court's recent ruling [in McDonald v. Chicago] notes that its decision does not necessarily strike down all local firearms regulations around the nation."

America

In the following viewpoint the editors of *America* contend that despite the 2010 US Supreme Court ruling on the right to keep and carry weapons, there is a need for regulation to minimize harm to society. The authors claim that although the Second Amendment may not allow an outright ban on all guns, it does allow localities to pass regulations to keep guns out of the hands of certain people. The authors suggest that given the statistics on gun deaths, more regulations are warranted.

America is a weekly Catholic magazine published by the Society of Jesus. Its editorial board is composed of Jesuit priests and brothers, as well as laypeople.

AS YOU READ, CONSIDER THE FOLLOWING QUESTIONS:

1. According to the authors, how did the US Supreme Court's ruling in *McDonald v. Chicago* (2010) differ from its ruling in *Heller v. District of Columbia* (2008)?
2. How many people die each year in America as a result of violence, killings, and suicide from guns, according to *America*?
3. According to the authors, American children under the age of fourteen are how many more times likely to be murdered by a gun than children in other industrialized nations?

The Supreme Court's 5-to-4 decision on June 28 [2010] in *McDonald v. Chicago* overturned that city's strict ban on handgun ownership. The ruling means that a homeowner may keep a handgun for self-defense. It marks a setback for gun control advocates and a victory for gun-rights proponents who claim that guns in the home make people safer. But the National Institute of Justice says the opposite, that keeping a gun in the home is associated with an increased risk of violent death by suicide or homicide and offers little protection from homicide at the hands of an intruder.

Unlike its 2008 ruling in *Heller v. District of Columbia*, which applied only to federal enclaves like the District, the court's current decision applies in all states and localities. But the court's recent ruling notes that its decision does not necessarily strike down all local firearms regulations around the nation. Writing for the majority in the recent ruling, Justice Samuel Alito observed that the Second Amendment right to keep and bear arms is not "a right to keep and carry any weapon whatsoever for whatsoever purpose," nor was the court questioning regulations such as those that prevent the mentally ill and felons from having guns. The 14th Amendment also entered into the decision, when Justice Alito wrote that the court's decision stemmed partly from the amendment, whose framers wanted to make sure that African Americans in the South could protect themselves from white supremacists.

Responding to the court's decision, Chicago mayor Richard Daley proposed alternative restrictions that he hopes will pass muster. In addition to requiring a firearms safety class and an exam, Daley's proposal bans gun shops in Chicago. It also prohibits gun owners from stepping outside their homes, even onto their own porch with a handgun. In Chicago, on the third weekend of this past June, the very month of the Supreme Court's decision, 50 people were shot; and seven of them died. Nationwide each year an average of 30,000 people die in gun violence, suicide and mass killings.

The Challenges to Gun Laws

But Chicago's new ordinance is already facing a lawsuit. The Illinois Association of Firearms Retailers has filed suit, alleging that the ordinance infringes on the residents' constitutional right to bear arms. The months and years ahead will bring many such challenges to local and state laws by gun-rights activists intent on overturning anti-gun ordinances. Kristen Rand, legislative director of the Violence Policy Center, has predicted that the litigation will "force cities, counties and states to expend scarce resources to defend longstanding, effective public safety laws." But she told *America* that many of the challenges will probably withstand judicial scrutiny. The reconstituted gun laws in the District of Columbia—close to what they were before the *Heller* case—now have restrictive licensing requirements "that discourage people from choosing to bring a gun into their home, and this has meant that comparatively few there have legally obtained handguns." The U.S. District Court has upheld the new ordinance.

> **FAST FACT**
>
> According to the Brady Campaign to Prevent Gun Violence, almost one hundred thousand people in America are shot or killed with a gun each year.

New York City's stringent gun laws are almost sure to be challenged, as are New Jersey's. The latter approved a law last year [2009] that prohibits individuals from purchasing more than one gun every 30 days. The New Jersey law also requires a prospective purchaser to obtain a police-issued permit for each handgun purchased and to undergo fingerprinting and background checks. On the West Coast, California also expects challenges by gun-rights groups. It has long had statewide restrictions on the sale and possession of military-style automatic weapons. Los Angeles' limits are among the most stringent: they ban the sale or transfer of easily concealed weapons and cheap handguns. Overall, the state's strict laws have proven successful. Since 1993, the mortality rate from gun-related deaths there has fallen 20 percent more than in the rest of the nation.

In response to the Supreme Court's decision in McDonald v. Chicago, *which struck down the city's gun ban, Chicago mayor Richard Daley (holding gun) proposed alternate restrictions, such as firearms safety classes and exams. His decision prompted more lawsuits.*

Gun Ownership and Gun Death Rates

The information in the selected states is listed in the following order:
· Rank in number of gun deaths
· Percentage of households owning guns
· Death rate from guns per 100,000 people

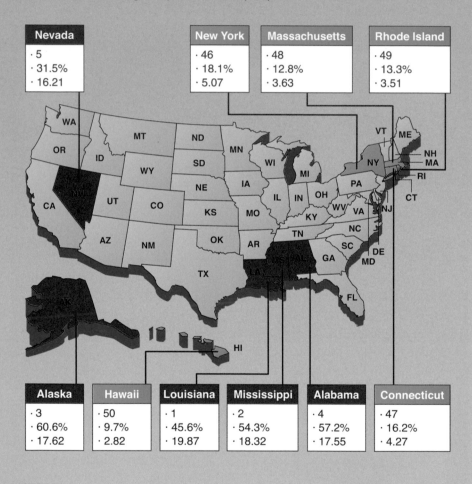

Nevada
· 5
· 31.5%
· 16.21

New York
· 46
· 18.1%
· 5.07

Massachusetts
· 48
· 12.8%
· 3.63

Rhode Island
· 49
· 13.3%
· 3.51

Alaska
· 3
· 60.6%
· 17.62

Hawaii
· 50
· 9.7%
· 2.82

Louisiana
· 1
· 45.6%
· 19.87

Mississippi
· 2
· 54.3%
· 18.32

Alabama
· 4
· 57.2%
· 17.55

Connecticut
· 47
· 16.2%
· 4.27

States with the Five *Highest* Gun Death Rates.

States with the Five *Lowest* Gun Death Rates.

Now, gun groups are intent on challenging restrictive laws around the nation and on expanding so-called open-carry and concealed weapons initiatives. The governor of Louisiana has signed into law a provision that allows people to carry handguns into churches. Virginia permits gun owners to carry their weapons into establishments that serve liquor. The gun violence prevention community is working to prevent such laws and to counter the gun lobby's illusory message that more guns make us safer. The Centers for Disease Control [and Prevention] has reported that American children age 14 and under are 16 times more likely than children in other industrialized nations to be murdered with a gun and 11 times more likely to commit suicide with a gun. Statistics like these suggest the need for more and better, rather than fewer and weaker, gun control laws.

EVALUATING THE AUTHOR'S ARGUMENTS:

In this viewpoint the editors of *America* claim that more gun control laws are needed. How would Robert A. Levy, author of the previous viewpoint, likely respond to their suggestion?

The Second Amendment Protects an Individual Right

"After a heyday from 1968 to 1990, the collective right theory met its ignominious end in 2008, collectively rejected by a unanimous Supreme Court."

Dave Kopel

In the following viewpoint Dave Kopel argues that the Second Amendment protects an individual right to keep and bear arms, not a collective right as it has sometimes been argued. Kopel claims that an anti-individual interpretation of the Second Amendment has been embraced in the past by lower courts, academics, and antigun activists. He contends that this wrongheaded interpretation has been forever put to rest by a 2008 US Supreme Court decision.

Kopel is the research director of the Independence Institute, an associate policy analyst at the Cato Institute, and an adjunct professor of advanced constitutional law at Denver University.

Dave Kopel, "Cooking Up a Collective Right: How a Mythical Monster Nearly Swallowed the Second Amendment Whole," *America's 1st Freedom,* September, 2011. Reproduced by permission of the author.

AS YOU READ, CONSIDER THE FOLLOWING QUESTIONS:
1. In what US Supreme Court decision was the collective right theory of the Second Amendment unanimously rejected, according to the author?
2. In what year did the anti-individual version of the Second Amendment gain traction within the Third Circuit Court of Appeals, according to Kopel?
3. What is the name of the legal scholar the author notes as an example of a scholar who studied the legal history of the Second Amendment?

E veryone knows the Second Amendment does not protect an individual right. Instead, it establishes a collective right, which cannot be legally asserted by an individual. The only people who claim the Second Amendment protects an individual right are deluded "gun nuts" who are ignorant of the original intent of the Second Amendment, and of the Supreme Court's past rulings.

If all you knew about the Second Amendment was what you learned from the national media, that's what you would have believed during the latter decades of the 20th century.

The *Heller* Opinion

Yet that view was entirely wrong, according to the *unanimous* Supreme Court in *District of Columbia v. Heller* (2008). How did such a foolish and obviously incorrect view of a constitutional right become so popular among America's opinion elite?

Let's start with some basic legal facts. In *Heller*, the five-justice majority led by Justice Antonin Scalia followed what is called the "standard model" of the Second Amendment—namely that the Second Amendment protects the right of all law-abiding persons to own, use and carry firearms for all legitimate purposes, especially for self-defense.

The four dissenting justices in *Heller*, led by Justice John Paul Stevens, instead preferred what is called the "narrow individual right." Under this theory, individuals have Second Amendment rights, but only in connection with service in a well-regulated militia.

Dick Anthony Heller (pictured) was the plaintiff in the case District of Columbia v. Heller, *which was heard in the US Supreme Court. The court's majority opinion stated that the Second Amendment protects the right of all law-abiding citizens to own, use, and carry firearms.*

The *Heller* dissenters did not elucidate the scope of the right, except that it did not include owning a handgun for personal self-defense.

According to Justice Stevens, "The question presented by this case is not whether the Second Amendment protects a 'collective right' or an 'individual right.' Surely it protects a right that can be enforced by individuals."

Justice Stephen Breyer wrote an additional dissent, which was joined by the same four justices who participated in the Stevens dissent. Justice Breyer wrote, "I take as a starting point the following four propositions, based on our precedent and today's opinions, to which I believe the entire Court subscribes: (1) The Amendment protects an 'individual' right—i.e. [that is], one that is separately possessed, and may be separately enforced, by each person on whom it is conferred."

So all nine justices agreed that the Second Amendment protects some sort of individual right. In contrast, the "collective right" theory asserts that there is *no* individual right. . . .

The Anti-Individual Collective Right

The U.S. Supreme Court ruled on the National Firearms Act in the 1939 case *United States v. Miller. Miller* is a confusing and opaque opinion, partly because it was written by the notoriously indolent [lazy] Justice James Clark McReynolds.

Nearly seven decades later, the justices in *Heller* argued vehemently about what *Miller* really meant. Justices Scalia and Stevens would each contend that *Miller* supported their own interpretation of the Second Amendment's individual right. Notably, not one of the *Heller* justices suggested that *Miller* stood for the anti-individual collective right.

The anti-individual version of the Second Amendment took a major step forward in 1942 when the federal Third Circuit Court of Appeals opined that the Second Amendment "was not adopted with individual rights in mind, but as a protection for the States in the maintenance of their militia organizations against possible encroachments by the federal power." *U.S. v. Tot.*

The states' right theory of the Third Circuit was not exactly the same as a collective right. The states' right, if taken seriously, would mean that the Second Amendment had somehow taken back some of the federal powers over state militias that had been granted by Article I of the U.S. Constitution. A states' rights Second Amendment would mean that state governments would have the power to negate federal gun control laws that applied to members of state militias. For example, a state government could declare that the state's militia consisted of all adults, and those militiamen (and militiawomen) should be able to own machine guns (or even grenades, bazookas, etc.) without federal taxation, registration or licensing.

The Pure Collective Right

In contrast, the pure collective right, as articulated by not-yet-impeached Judge [Halsted] Ritter, seemed to mean a "right" that could be exercised neither by an individual nor by a state government.

Like "collective property" in a communist dictatorship, the collective right to arms supposedly belonged to everybody at once, but not to individuals or state governments. Thus, the "right" actually belonged to nobody and nothing, and had no practical existence.

This was the theory of the influential public intellectual Garry Wills, who insisted that only "wacky scholars" believed that the Second Amendment protects an individual right. According to Wills, the Second Amendment "had no real meaning." Instead, James Madison's "shrewd ploy" had created an entire constitutional amendment with no substantive content.

As gun control became a major issue in the 1960s, and gun prohibition began to appear politically realistic, the nihilist collective right theory began to catch on. The New Jersey Supreme Court was the first to actually use the term "collective right," when in 1968 it upheld the state's then-new gun licensing statute in *Burton v. Sills*. Quoting a 1966 article from the *Northwestern Law Review*, the New Jersey court stated that the Second Amendment "was not framed with Individual rights in mind. Thus it refers to the collective right 'of the people' to keep and bear arms in connection with 'a well-regulated militia.'"

Meanwhile, in intellectual circles, the "collective right" was becoming the easy way to sneeringly dismiss anyone who raised constitutional objections to gun prohibition. At the time, there was little scholarly research on the Second Amendment. The legal history of the Founding era and the 19th century had become obscure or forgotten. . . .

The Second Amendment in the Courts

The Gun Control Act of 1968 vastly expanded the scope of federal gun laws. Soon, the federal courts were hearing plenty of cases about "prohibited persons" (usually convicted felons) who had violated federal law by possessing a firearm. The factual guilt of these defendants was indisputable, so their attorneys sometimes resorted to the desperate argument that the gun ban violated the felons' Second Amendment rights.

The federal district courts and courts of appeal unanimously rejected such arguments. As Justice Scalia's majority opinion in *Heller* affirmed, recognizing the right of law-abiding Americans to possess guns does not require allowing convicted felons, or the insane, to have guns.

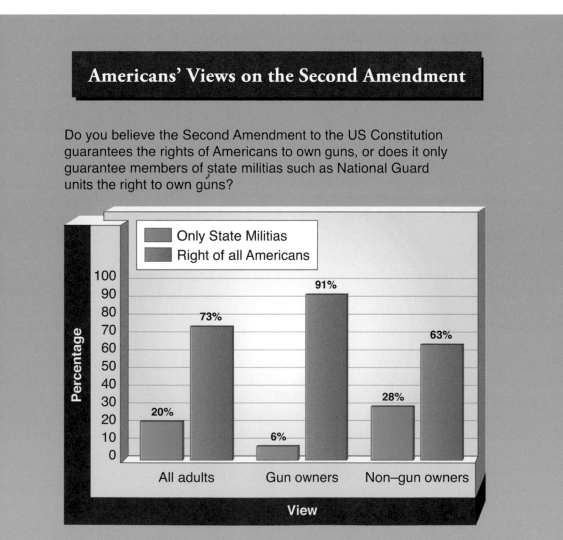

Americans' Views on the Second Amendment

Do you believe the Second Amendment to the US Constitution guarantees the rights of Americans to own guns, or does it only guarantee members of state militias such as National Guard units the right to own guns?

Taken from: "*USA Today*/Gallup Poll of 1,016 Adults," February 8–10, 2008. www.usatoday.com.

However, the federal courts tended to go much further. Some courts used a very narrow version of the "narrow individual right" (e.g., the defendant was possessing the gun for personal use, and not for militia service, and therefore he cannot rely on the Second Amendment). Other courts declared that the Second Amendment was a state's right. Still others ruled that the Second Amendment was a collective right.

The judicial opinions frequently made little distinction between the different theories, and addressed the Second Amendment dismissively. Although the American people continued to believe that the Second Amendment guaranteed their individual right to own firearms for self-defense, hunting, target shooting and other legitimate uses, the collective right theory became supreme in the national media, in academic circles and among gun-banning politicians.

The Historical Rediscovery of the Second Amendment

Yet the collective-right theory itself contained the seeds of its own destruction. Emboldened by the collective right's negation of the Second Amendment, politicians and gun-ban lobbies intensified the pressure for draconian gun control, and so scholars began looking into the actual legal history of the Second Amendment. One such scholar was a University of Arizona Law School student named David Hardy. His 1974 article in the *Chicago-Kent Law Review*, "Of Arms and the Law," marked the beginning of the historical rediscovery of the Second Amendment.

For a while, the legal academy tried to ignore the mounting historical evidence that the Second Amendment protects an individual right. But in 1989, left-leaning University of Texas professor Sanford Levinson penned "The Embarrassing Second Amendment" for the *Yale Law Journal.* Levinson suggested that law professors and the rest of the elite bar had avoided looking carefully at the Second Amendment because of "a mixture of sheer opposition to the idea of private ownership of guns and the perhaps subconscious fear that altogether plausible, perhaps even 'winning,' interpretations of the Second Amendment would present real hurdles to those of us supporting prohibitory regulation."

With Levinson having legitimated scholarly inquiry, what had once been a trickle of scholarship turned into a flood. The "collective right" became increasingly implausible. . . .

An End to the Collective Right Theory

Rather obdurately [stubbornly], the [Bill] Clinton administration clung to the most anti-individual theory possible. In the 2000 oral argument of *United States v. Emerson* before the 5th Circuit, the Clinton administration insisted that there was no individual Second Amendment right at all; the federal government could even disarm a state National Guardsman in active service.

By the time *Heller* was being briefed in early 2008, the collective right theory had all but vanished, at least among experts. Of the *amicus* briefs filed in support of the D.C. handgun ban, only one made an extended argument for the collective right. That brief came from Bill Clinton's former Attorney General Janet Reno, Barack Obama's future Attorney General Eric Holder and some other former officials.

After a heyday from 1968 to 1990, the collective right theory met its ignominious end in 2008, collectively rejected by a unanimous Supreme Court. It was a well-deserved demise of a theory that never should have gained traction, yet did so anyway because of dishonest judicial decisions and gun-ban proponents who repeated the lies until some actually came to believe they were true.

EVALUATING THE AUTHOR'S ARGUMENTS:

In this viewpoint Dave Kopel argues that the Second Amendment "right of the people to keep and bear arms" applies to individuals, not collectively to the people. How might an opponent of this view argue that the Second Amendment is not meant to apply to individuals?

The Second Amendment Does Not Protect an Individual Right

John Massaro

> *"The Second Amendment has nothing to do with the private possession and carriage of weapons."*

In the following viewpoint John Massaro claims that most people, including the justices of the US Supreme Court, are wrong in their interpretation of the Second Amendment as referring to an individual right. Massaro contends that the wording of the Second Amendment clearly refers to the right of the general populace to store weapons related to use by the militia and takes no position whatsoever on the individual right to keep and bear arms.

Massaro is the writer and the editor of the website SoapboxWeekly.com and author of *No Guarantee of a Gun: How and Why the Second Amendment Means Exactly What It Says.*

John Massaro, "The High Court Incorporated the Wrong Second Amendment Right," *Progressive Populist,* September 1, 2010. Reproduced by permission of the author.

1. Massaro claims that the individual right to possess and carry weapons was created by the US Supreme Court in what case?
2. According to the author, how are the terms *people*, *persons*, and *person*, used in the US Constitution?
3. The author claims that gun control is not a matter of law, but a matter of what?

The Second Amendment is unique in American law in that virtually all case law and all commentary on the subject are wrong. Reasons for the controversy over the Second Amendment are politics and reliance on its erroneous case law and flawed commentary as authority. In its recent decision in *McDonald v. City of Chicago* [2010], the Supreme Court overturned both *United States v. Cruikshank* (1876) and *Presser v. Illinois* (1886) and correctly incorporated the Second Amendment through the Fourteenth Amendment to apply to states and localities. However, the right that was incorporated was the right of the individual to possess and carry weapons that was created by the Court in *District of Columbia, v. Heller* (2008) and not the original and, therefore, correct right of the general populace to store weapons and render military service as the Organized State Militia that is today known as the National Guard, which is the right that the Founders drafted in 1789 and the states ratified and the nation adopted in 1791. Therefore, as strange as it might sound, in *McDonald*, the correct holding of the Supreme Court should have been that a state or local law that regulates the possession and carriage of weapons is Constitutional; that the Second Amendment right that must be incorporated through the Fourteenth Amendment to apply to states and localities is the right of the general populace to store weapons and render military service as the Organized State Militia that is known today as the National Guard; and that the Second Amendment has nothing to do with the private possession and carriage of weapons. . . .

A Misunderstanding of the Second Amendment

Both sides in *McDonald* joined the Supreme Court in approaching the case from a fundamental misunderstanding of the Second

Timeline of Important Second Amendment Court Decisions

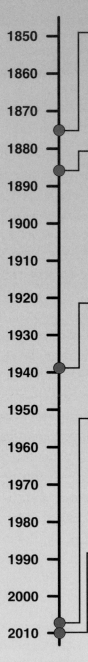

1850	
1860	
1870	
1880	
1890	
1900	
1910	
1920	
1930	
1940	
1950	
1960	
1970	
1980	
1990	
2000	
2010	

1875 — United States v. Cruikshank

The court rules that it is up to the states, not the federal government, to protect the fundamental rights of citizens, saying that the Second Amendment "has no other effect than to restrict the powers of the national government."

1886 — Presser v. Illinois

The court reaffirms that the Second Amendment only restricts the power of the federal government and has the following comment on bearing arms: "It is undoubtedly true that all citizens capable of bearing arms constitute the reserved military force or reserve militia of the United States as well as of the states."

1939 — United States v. Miller

The court declines to offer Second Amendment constitutional protection to a particular type of gun since it does not have "some reasonable relationship to the preservation or efficiency of a well regulated militia."

2008 — District of Columbia v. Heller

The court rules that the Second Amendment gives gun ownership rights to individuals within federal enclaves, striking down parts of the Firearms Control Regulations Act of 1975 that banned residents of the District of Columbia from owning handguns and other firearms.

2010 — McDonald v. City of Chicago

The court ruled that gun ownership rights guaranteed by the Second Amendment are also protected from state interference, parting ways with the reasoning used in nineteenth-century cases.

[Compiled by editor.]

Amendment. *Heller* marked the first time since *United States v. Miller* (1939) that the Court ruled directly and specifically on the Second Amendment. The Court's opinion in *Heller* revealed that some members of the Court have a bunker mentality about the Second Amendment, and all nine justices, those of both the dissent and the majority, misinterpreted the Second Amendment. Nevertheless, the District of Columbia in *Heller* and Chicago in *McDonald* were represented by attorneys who might be fine attorneys otherwise but were totally incompetent with regard to the Second Amendment. . . .

Proper study of the Second Amendment does not adhere to false theories or attempt the futile task of trying to reconcile the "Militia Clause" and the "Bear Arms Clause," as the individual-right and state-right theories try to do (and the Supreme Court has tried to do), and reveals that the original and correct understanding of the Second Amendment runs counter to virtually all case law and all commentary on the subject. Despite the fact that highly trained attorneys and even the justices of the highest court in the nation do not understand the Second Amendment, the Second Amendment is what it is, which is what it always has been, no matter what jurists, scholars, and activists attempt to make it out to be. Correct interpretation of the Second Amendment requires defining its actual terms. And in accordance with Constitutional originalism, definitions of the terms must be as they were understood by the Founders and not as they are understood by Twenty-First Century Americans. Even a brief summary of the original and correct interpretation of the Second Amendment contains irrefutable documentary evidence that was never brought to the attention of the Supreme Court by the incompetent (with regard to the Second Amendment) attorneys that have argued Second Amendment cases before it. Therefore, any disagreement with this interpretation of the Second Amendment (which is that of the Founders) means disagreeing with the Founders. Everyone is entitled to his own opinion on guns, but no one is entitled to his own historical facts, no matter what the Supreme Court says.

Definition of Second Amendment Terms

Understanding the Second Amendment requires understanding four points. The first point is that "A well regulated Militia" refers to the Organized State Militia that is today known as the National Guard and not to individuals who are proficient in the use of weapons or to the entire population. . . .

The next point is that "people" refers to the general populace and not to individuals. In the unamended Constitution, the original amendments, and the modern amendments, the Framers used "people" to describe the general populace, "persons" to describe individuals, and "person" to describe an individual. The unamended Constitution uses "people" 2 times, uses "persons" 4 times, and uses "person" 16 times. One must agree that although "persons" is the plural of "person," "people" must mean something different than "persons," or the Founders would not have used both terms. For example, in the unamended Constitution, the right of electing House members is that of the people (the general populace). Election by the people means by the general populace. After all, not every individual votes for the winner of the election not every individual votes in the election, and not every individual is even eligible to vote in the election to begin with. . . .

In addition, since "people" refers to the general populace and not to individuals, "keep" refers to the storage of weapons by the general populace and not to the private possession of weapons by individuals. This is not inconsistent with the rest of the Constitution. The term "keep" is used twice in the unamended Constitution; in neither Article I, Section 5, Clause 3 nor Article I, Section 10, Clause 3 does "keep" in any way connote personal private possession. In the Second Amendment, "keep" refers to the storage of weapons by the general populace. This connotation of "keep" is perpetuated in modern state statutes that provide for the keeping (storage) of National Guard weapons in public depositories (armories). . . .

The Second Amendment and Gun Control

Fourth, "bear Arms" means "render military service" and not "carry weapons." Conclusive evidence of this term's true meaning comes from The *Federalist Papers*, the *Anti-Federalist papers*, and early state constitutions that were adopted before the United States Constitution. In *The Federalist 46*, James Madison, the original author of the Second Amendment, clearly states that one-quarter of the population is "able to bear arms." (He states that the 25,000–30,000 persons ("one hundredth part of the whole number of souls") in a regular army are "one twenty-fifth part of the number able to bear arms.") This makes sense only when it means that one quarter of the population is "able to render military service" and can indicate only that one quarter of the population—that is, those who were able-bodied males, since they were the ones who were "able to bear arms" ("able to render military service")—is "able to bear arms," as in "able to render military service." If Madison's connotation of "able to bear arms" were "able to carry weapons," then he would be saying that only one quarter of the population is "able to carry weapons." That connotation would make for a population in which three quarters are so physically handicapped that they are not "able to carry weapons." Even the three quarters of the population (women, children, and the aged) that are not "able to

National Guardsmen are pictured here. Proponents of gun control contend that the Second Amendment refers to the right of the general populace to store weapons for use in military service, such as the National Guard, and that the amendment does not apply to the individual right to keep and bear arms.

bear arms" ("able to render military service") would be "able to carry weapons" as long as they have the mere ability to grip and transport a gun (that is, anyone who had hands that could grip and was able to walk would have been "able to carry weapons"). It is simply not plausible that three quarters of Americans were that severely handicapped back in 1787 or 1788. . . .

The truth about the Second Amendment signifies that gun control is a public-policy issue and not a justiciable one. The Second Amendment has absolutely no relevance to gun control. For too long, gun control has been incorrectly dichotomized into policy and law. Part of the debate has focused on what, if any, gun-control laws would be good public policy. But part of the debate has incorrectly focused on the extent to which guns can be regulated without violating a supposed individual Second Amendment right to possess and carry weapons. However, proof that the Second Amendment does not guarantee any individual right to possess and carry weapons can move the debate on gun control out of its erroneous context of Constitutional law and leave it solely in its correct context of public policy. The nation could then focus exclusively on what laws would be in the public interest without worrying that a law that might be good policy might be in violation of the Second Amendment or the Fourteenth Amendment. (Whether or not the Ninth Amendment, the Tenth Amendment, or any other part of the Constitution besides the Second Amendment and the Fourteenth Amendment guarantees an individual right to possess and carry weapons is completely outside the scope of the Second Amendment.)

EVALUATING THE AUTHOR'S ARGUMENTS:

In this viewpoint John Massaro says that whereas gun control is a matter of opinion, the meaning of the Second Amendment is bound by historical facts. How might an opponent of Massaro's viewpoint object to his method of interpreting the Second Amendment?

Viewpoint

5

The Second Amendment Protects the People from Government

"When the government ignores the First Amendment, it is time to rattle the Second Amendment sabers."

Skip Coryell

In the following viewpoint Skip Coryell claims that the right to possess and use firearms is an important equalizing force between citizens and criminals, and citizens and government. Coryell contends that although the First Amendment right to free speech is an important method of petitioning the government, the people need the Second Amendment right to bear arms in case the government fails to listen to them.

Coryell is a writer and a Certified National Rifle Association Pistol Instructor and Chief Range Safety Officer.

AS YOU READ, CONSIDER THE FOLLOWING QUESTIONS:

1. Coryell claims that without the right to keep and bear arms, society would revert to the default state of what?
2. The author refers to what historical event as explanation for why the Founding Fathers created the Second Amendment?
3. Coryell claims that it is time to use the force of the Second Amendment when government ignores what?

Skip Coryell, "Rattling the Second Amendment Saber," *Human Events,* March 23, 2010. Copyright © 2010 Human Events Inc. All rights reserved. Reproduced by permission.

According to *Webster's New World College Dictionary*, the term "saber rattling" is defined as: *a threatening of war, or a menacing show of armed force.*

Some people call it posturing. In the animal world it's related to establishing "pecking order." Some people would have us believe that a pecking order is a bad thing, that it's barbaric, and should be reserved only for the animal world. I disagree. It's a natural thing that will happen no matter how much people try to suppress it. Pecking order keeps the world in a state of organized cosmos. Every playground has one, every corporate board room, and even the halls of Congress. It's the way the world works, and without it there would be chaos and unending strife. People have to know who is in charge and who must bend the knee and kiss the ring that rules.

The Need for Firearms

I suppose that's why firearms are so important. They are the equalizing force, available to all free people everywhere. They tell the 200-pound sexually aggressive male that he must not rape the 120-pound female, who is alone on the street at night with no one around to protect her. The firearm gives her the ability to kill the stronger male.

Firearms tell the sociopath that he must not break into your family's home at night and kill your family as you sleep. There is always the chance that you will awaken, get your firearm and shoot him until he dies. Dead sociopaths and dead rapists. That's a good thing, a necessary thing for society to function in an orderly fashion.

Without the right to keep and bear arms, we revert to humanity's default state of "law of the jungle," where only the strong survive, where the big rule the small, and where the weak die in a puddle of blood, flesh and urine. We need the firearm and the freedom to use it or our children will live in a binary world of masters and slaves, with no check on immorality, no governor to hold the strong accountable, and no way to protect the weak from the strong.

In a world without freedom and firearms, only the evil will have guns, and they will use them to the detriment and enslavement of good people everywhere. History has taught us that, and it's a lesson we should forget only at our own peril.

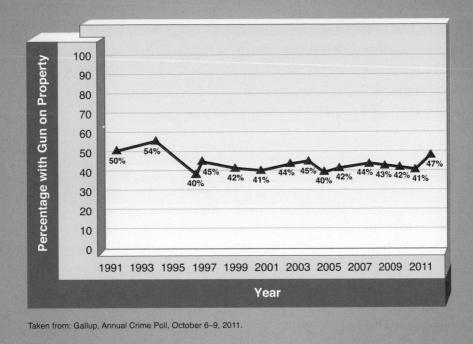

American Gun Households, 1991–2011

Taken from: Gallup, Annual Crime Poll, October 6–9, 2011.

The Use of the First Amendment

So what does all this have to do with saber rattling, a threatening of war, or a menacing show of armed force?

Look at the present situation in America. Many say we are on the brink of economic collapse. Our elected officials exude an unprecedented arrogance, totally ignoring the will of the people, hell-bent on dragging us into a world we neither want for ourselves nor our children. In short, the pecking order has been established, and it's 180 degrees out of phase. They are the ruling class and we are subservient to them.

Or are we?

I hear the clank of metal on metal in the distance.

All across the country, Americans are rising up and biting the hand that feeds them. In some cases, the hand is getting ripped clean off! In Virginia, in New Jersey, and even in Massachusetts. The chain is chafing their necks and they want it gone!

The politicians—they ignore us.

For the past year [2009–2010] we've heard a lot about the TEA parties and the nine-twelvers. People like [conservative commentator] Glenn Beck (God bless him) continue to educate America on Freedom 101 and the original intent of our founding fathers. We the people have been exercising our First Amendment rights to the hilt. We're screaming! We're protesting! We're faxing! We're phoning and marching and yelling. . . .

But still—they ignore us.

I hear the clank of metal on metal in the distance, but not so distant today as it was yesterday or the day before, or the day before, or the day before.

I have a feeling, just a feeling, that I'm not alone. There are a lot of people out there like me who will no longer tolerate the arrogance of politicians who ignore us. I've been told that there's only one thing worse than being abused, and that's being ignored. If you kick me, at least I know I exist. But if you ignore me, then I'm not even worth the trouble.

And here's the million-dollar question: "What happens if the First Amendment fails?"

Our founding fathers answered that when the King of England ignored their pleas for fairness, for equal representation, and for basic human rights. The founders rattled their sabers for years, hoping above hope that they would never have to use them. But, in the end, the King acted like a King and tried to dominate and disarm his disloyal subjects.

The Use of Weapons

Several years ago, I was teaching a husband and wife in a private firearms class. We were on the range behind their barn, shooting at targets up against an embankment. The woman was shooting a nice, 9mm Glock, and she honestly could not hit the broad side of a barn from the inside. I tried everything I knew to get her on target, but it was no use. I couldn't find the problem. Her husband told me she was a good shot, and that she usually shot better than he did. I questioned her some more, and she finally threw up her hands in frustration and said, "I don't even know why I'm doing this! I could never shoot anyone anyways. My husband made me take this class!" At her remark, a light went off in my head, and I interjected. "What if someone was trying to kill you? Could you shoot someone then?" She said, "No! I couldn't kill someone to save my own life. I'd just go ahead and die!"

I thought that was rather odd, but I could tell she was sincere, so I thought about it a second, and then I said.

"Okay, let's use a little training technique called visualization."

She nodded her head impatiently.

"Okay, here's the scenario: You're at the gas station filling your tank. A man drives up and parks next to your car. He gets out, walks over, reaches through the open window of your car, removes your daughter from her car seat and puts her in his own vehicle. He then starts to get into his car to drive away."

There was a horrified look on the young mother's face.

"At that moment in time, could you take another human life?"

Without hesitation, this proper Christian woman said, "I would kill that son of a bitch!"

I said, "Okay then, that target down there is the man who is stealing your daughter. Fire away." She never missed the target again.

The Use of Force Against the Government

My question to everyone reading this article is this: "For you, as an individual, when do you draw your saber? When do you say 'Yes, I am willing to rise up and overthrow an oppressive, totalitarian government?'"

Is it when the government takes away your private business?

Is it when the government rigs elections?

Is it when the government imposes martial law?

Is it when the government takes away your firearms?

Now, don't get me wrong. I'm not advocating the immediate use of force against the government. It isn't time, and hopefully that time will never come. But one thing is certain: "Now is the time to rattle your sabers." If not now, then when?

Opponents of gun control believe the right to possess and use firearms is an important equalizing force between citizens and government and between citizens and criminals.

When the government ignores the First Amendment, it is time to rattle the Second Amendment sabers. It's all about accountability. So long as our elected officials believe we will rise up and overthrow them under certain conditions, then they will not allow those conditions to occur. Their jobs and their very lives depend on it.

I understand that sounds harsh, but these are harsh times. Now is the time to rattle the saber. Now is the time to answer the very personal, very serious, very intimate question: "When do I remove the saber from its scabbard?"

I hear the clank of metal on metal getting closer, but that's not enough. The politicians have to hear it too. They have to hear it, and they have to believe it.

EVALUATING THE AUTHOR'S ARGUMENTS:

In this viewpoint Skip Coryell encourages the rattling of "Second Amendment sabers." What exactly do you think he is encouraging?

The Second Amendment Does Not Allow Citizens to Threaten Government

"The Second Amendment now securely holds a right to personal self-defense against assault, but not against the obligations of citizenship."

Garrett Epps

In the following viewpoint Garrett Epps argues that the purpose of the Second Amendment is not to arm citizens so that they can intimidate government and limit its power. Epps claims that there is no historical evidence for the idea that the Framers of the Constitution would have wanted the Second Amendment to support the threat of violence by sovereign citizens, and he warns that civil society is threatened by the notion that it does.

Epps is a professor of law at the University of Baltimore School of Law and the author of *Democracy Reborn: The Fourteenth Amendment and the Fight for Equal Rights in Post–Civil War America.*

Garrett Epps, "Constitutional Myth #6: The Second Amendment Allows Citizens to Threaten Government," *Atlantic,* June 30, 2011. Reproduced by permission of the author.

1. What quote does the author claim has been misattributed to President Thomas Jefferson?
2. What reason does the author give for thinking that the Framers of the US Constitution and the Bill of Rights had few illusions about the virtues of violence?
3. What three rights does Epps give as examples of rights that are subject to reasonable regulation?

I n 2008, the Supreme Court recognized—for the first time in American history—the "right to bear arms" as a personal, individual right, permitting law-abiding citizens to possess handguns in their home for their personal protection. Two years later, it held that both state and federal governments must observe this newly discovered right.

Two Fallacies About Gun Rights

Curiously enough, the far-right responded to these radical victories as if the sky had fallen. During hearings on the nomination of Elena Kagan to the Supreme Court, Alabama Sen. Jeff Sessions direly warned that the two gun cases—*Heller v. District of Columbia* and *McDonald v. City of Chicago*—were 5–4 decisions. "Our Second Amendment rights are hanging by a thread," he said. The idea that the rights of ordinary gun owners are in danger is a fallacy.

A second, and more pernicious, fallacy is embodied by this quotation from Thomas Jefferson, America's third president: "When governments fear the people, there is liberty. When the people fear the government, there is tyranny. The strongest reason for the people to retain the right to keep and bear arms is, as a last resort, to protect themselves against tyranny in government."

Wait a minute, Epps! Who could argue with Jefferson? Well, not me, to be sure. But there's a problem with this quote, as there is with so much of the rhetoric about the Second Amendment.

It's false.

As far as scholars can tell, Jefferson never said it. Monticello.org, the official website of the Thomas Jefferson Foundation, says, "We have

"US's loose gun laws," cartoon by Manny Francisco, January 16, 2011, www.CagleCartoons.com. Copyright © 2011 by Manny Francisco, www.CagleCartoons.com. All rights reserved. Reproduced by permission.

not found any evidence that Thomas Jefferson said or wrote, 'When governments fear the people, there is liberty. When the people fear the government, there is tyranny,' or any of its listed variations." The quotation (which has also been misattributed to Samuel Adams, Thomas Paine, and *The Federalist*), actually was apparently said in 1914 by the eminent person-no-one's-ever-heard-of John Basil Barnhill, during a debate in St. Louis.

As bogus as the quote is the idea that the purpose of the Second Amendment was to create a citizenry able to intimidate the government, and that America would be a better place if government officials were to live in constant fear of gun violence. If good government actually came from a violent, armed population, then Afghanistan and Somalia would be the two best-governed places on earth. As we saw from the 2010 shootings in Tucson, Arizona, [of congresswoman Gabrielle Giffords, Judge John Roll, and seventeen others] the consequences for democracy of guns in private hands, without reasonable regulation, can be dire—a society where a member of Congress cannot meet constituents without suffering traumatic brain injury [as did Giffords], and where a federal judge cannot stop by a meeting on his way back from Mass without being shot dead [as was Roll].

But that image of a *Mad Max* republic lives on in the fringes of the national imagination. It is what authors Joshua Horwitz and Casey Anderson call "the insurrectionist idea," the notion that the Constitution enshrines an individual right to nullify laws an armed citizen objects to. Its most prominent recent expression came from Senate candidate Sharon Angle, who predicted that if she was unable to defeat Democratic Sen. Harry Reid at the ballot box (which she couldn't), citizens would turn to "Second Amendment remedies"—in essence, assassination. Rand Paul also likes to hint that the remedy for rejection of his libertarian policies may be hot lead. Deathandtaxesmag. com quotes him as saying, "Some citizens are holding out hope that the upcoming elections will better things. We'll wait and see. Lots of us believe that maybe that's unreliable considering that the Fabian progressive socialists have been chipping at our foundations for well over 100 years. Regardless, the founders made sure we had Plan B: the Second Amendment."

The History and Meaning of the Second Amendment

The history and meaning of the Second Amendment are a murky subject. A fair reading of the entire text of the Constitution suggests that the most prominent concern of the its framers was protecting states' control of their militias. Under Article I § 8 of the Constitution, the states transferred to Congress the power "to provide for calling forth the militia to execute the laws of the union, suppress insurrections and repel Invasions" and "to provide for organizing, arming, and disciplining, the militia." This was one of the most radical features of the original Constitution; under the Articles of Confederation, states had complete control of their militias. Opponents of ratification suggested that the new federal government might proceed to disarm and dissolve the state militias and create instead a national standing army. The Second Amendment most clearly addresses that concern; and that has led a number of historians to suggest that the Amendment really has no relation to any personal right of individuals to "keep and bear arms."

History is rarely that clear, however, and the notion of personal gun possession as a right is also deeply rooted in American history. UCLA Law Professor Adam Winkler, author of the [book] *Gunfight: The Battle over the Right to Bear Arms in America*, notes that since before the Amendment was proposed, many citizens have discussed the right to bear arms as a guarantee against tyranny as well as a feature of a federal system. Indeed, Winkler's reading of the history finds more support for this anti-tyranny idea than for the Supreme Court's current doctrine that the Second Amendment supports a right of personal self-defense. But the protection against tyranny was a long-term structural guarantee, not a privilege of individual nullification, he says. "I

The 2011 shooting of US representative Gabrielle Giffords, Judge John Roll, and seventeen others has been cited by gun control advocates as proof that an armed citizenry can be dangerous in the extreme.

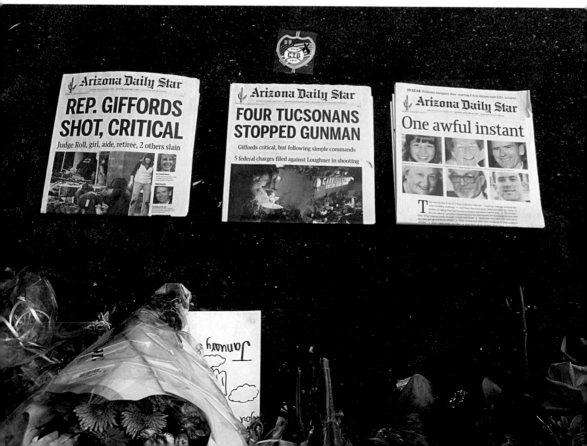

don't think there's any support for the idea that government officials should be afraid of being shot."

It would be odd indeed if the Framers of the Constitution and the Bill of Rights had written an amendment designed to give individuals the right to liquidate the government they were setting up. In fact, having been through a revolution, they had few illusions about the virtues of violence. When they gathered in Philadelphia in 1787, the original Framers were very aware that armed bands of farmers in Massachusetts had revolted against the state government only a few months earlier. [George] Washington, in particular, found the news of Daniel Shays's rebellion in that state so disturbing that it contributed to his decision to come out of retirement and help frame a new national charter to prevent such outbreaks.

The Issue of Rebellion

At Philadelphia, Gouverneur [Morris]of Pennsylvania warned the delegates that failure would precipitate new outbreaks of rebellion. "The scenes of horror attending civil commotion cannot be described, and the conclusion of them will be worse than the term of their continuance," he said. "The stronger party will then make traitors of the weaker; and the gallows & halter will finish the work of the sword."

After becoming President, Washington himself led a national army into Western Pennsylvania to suppress a rebellion against the new federal tax on whiskey. (This is the only time in American history a President has served as Commander-in-Chief *in the field*.) In a subsequent message to Congress, he showed precious little sympathy for "Second Amendment remedies:"

> [T]o yield to the treasonable fury of so small a portion of the United States, would be to violate the fundamental principle of our constitution, which enjoins that the will of the majority shall prevail. . . . [S]ucceeding intelligence has tended to manifest the necessity of what has been done; it being now confessed by those who were not inclined to exaggerate the ill-conduct of the insurgents, that their malevolence was not pointed merely to a particular law; but that a spirit, inimical to all order, has actuated many of the offenders.

In 2011, there is abroad in the land "a spirit, inimical to all order," particularly if that order concerns federally guaranteed environmental protection, economic regulation, or civil rights. Voices from the far-right are trying to plant a parasitic meme in our Bill of Rights: that America is not a self-government republic, but a dark Hobbesian [after political philosopher Thomas Hobbes] plane where each "sovereign citizen" chooses what laws to obey, and any census taker or federal law-enforcement agent had better beware. The long-term result of such a "right to bear arms" would be an ungovernable state of nature, where life, both civic and individual, would be solitary, poor, nasty, brutish and short [as Hobbes put it].

The Second Amendment now securely holds a right to personal self-defense against assault, but not against the obligations of citizenship. A right of self-defense, like the right of free speech, or the right to be secure against unreasonable searches, is subject to reasonable regulation. Common-sense concern with the consequences of legal rules, not chest-thumping about squirrel rifles and the Revolutionary War, will produce a system of laws that would recognize the nation's heritage of gun ownership, and allow reasonable regulations to protect us all from Somalia-style chaos.

EVALUATING THE AUTHOR'S ARGUMENTS:

In this viewpoint Garrett Epps claims that the Second Amendment is not meant to be used by individuals to intimidate government. Given Epps's position, do you think he would agree more with Dave Kopel or with John Massaro, authors of previous viewpoints in this chapter, on the issue of whether or not the Second Amendment protects an individual right? Explain your reasoning.

Chapter 2

What Gun Control Regulations Are Effective and Necessary?

A Providence, Rhode Island police officer displays a seized assault weapon. Police organizations overwhelmingly back bans on assault weapons.

Viewpoint 1

What Happened to the Ban on Assault Weapons?

"The White House and Congress must not give up on trying to reinstate a ban on assault weapons, even if it may be politically difficult."

Jimmy Carter

In the following viewpoint Jimmy Carter argues that the ban on assault weapons should be restored. Carter claims that assault weapons are importantly different from other weapons protected by the Second Amendment right to bear arms. Carter contends that most Americans support an assault weapon ban and that the consequences of not banning these weapons are deadly.

Carter, the thirty-ninth president of the United States, is founder of the Jimmy and Rosalyn Carter Center, which works to advance global efforts to wage peace, fight disease, and build hope.

AS YOU READ, CONSIDER THE FOLLOWING QUESTIONS:
1. What three examples of semiautomatic assault weapons does Carter give?
2. The author claims that many hunters do not support the extreme policies of what gun-rights group?
3. In 2005, according to Carter, a child or teenager was killed in a firearm-related accident or suicide how frequently?

The evolution in public policy concerning the manufacture, sale and possession of semiautomatic assault weapons like AK-47s, AR-15s and Uzis has been very disturbing. Presidents Ronald Reagan, George H.W. Bush, Bill Clinton and I all supported a ban on these formidable firearms, and one was finally passed in 1994.

When the 10-year ban was set to expire, many police organizations—including 1,100 police chiefs and sheriffs from around the nation—called on Congress and President George W. Bush to renew and strengthen it. But with a wink from the White House, the gun lobby prevailed and the ban expired.

President Bill Clinton (pictured) speaks to law enforcement officials at the White House in 1994 about his proposed assault weapons ban. Presidents Jimmy Carter, Ronald Reagan, and George H.W. Bush have all supported assault weapons bans.

I have used weapons since I was big enough to carry one, and now own two handguns, four shotguns and three rifles, two with scopes. I use them carefully, for hunting game from our family woods and fields, and occasionally for hunting with my family and friends in other places. We cherish the right to own a gun and some of my hunting companions like to collect rare weapons. One of them is a superb craftsman who makes muzzle-loading rifles, one of which I displayed for four years in my private White House office.

But none of us wants to own an assault weapon, because we have no desire to kill policemen or go to a school or workplace to see how many victims we can accumulate before we are finally shot or take our own lives. That's why the White House and Congress must not give up on trying to reinstate a ban on assault weapons, even if it may be politically difficult.

An overwhelming majority of Americans, including me and my hunting companions, believe in the right to own weapons, but surveys show that they also support modest restraints like background checks, mandatory registration and brief waiting periods before purchase.

> ## FAST FACT
>
> The Federal Assault Weapons Ban expired on September 13, 2004, and although there have been multiple attempts to renew the ban, no bill has reached the floor for a vote as of May 2012.

A majority of Americans also support banning assault weapons. Many of us who hunt are dismayed by some of the more extreme policies of the National Rifle Association, the most prominent voice in opposition to a ban, and by the timidity of public officials who yield to the group's unreasonable demands.

Heavily influenced and supported by the firearms industry, N.R.A. leaders have misled many gullible people into believing that our weapons are going to be taken away from us, and that homeowners will be deprived of the right to protect ourselves and our families. The N.R.A. would be justified in its efforts if there was a real threat to our constitutional right to bear arms. But that is not the case.

Instead, the N.R.A. is defending criminals' access to assault weapons and use of ammunition that can penetrate protective clothing

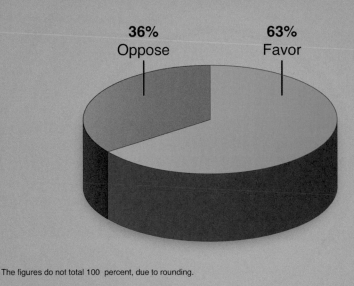

American Opinion on a Nationwide Assault Weapons Ban, 2011

36%
Oppose

63%
Favor

The figures do not total 100 percent, due to rounding.

Taken from: CBS News/*New York Times* poll, January 15–19, 2011.

worn by police officers on duty. In addition, while the N.R.A. seems to have reluctantly accepted current law restricting sales by licensed gun dealers to convicted felons, it claims that only "law-abiding people" obey such restrictions—and it opposes applying them to private gun dealers or those who sell all kinds of weapons from the back of a van or pickup truck at gun shows.

What are the results of this profligate ownership and use of guns designed to kill people? In 2006, the Centers for Disease Control and Prevention reported more than 30,000 people died from firearms, accounting for nearly 20 percent of all injury deaths. In 2005, every nine hours a child or teenager in the United States was killed in a firearm-related accident or suicide.

Across our border, Mexican drug cartels are being armed with advanced weaponry imported from the United States—a reality only the N.R.A. seems to dispute.

The gun lobby and the firearms industry should reassess their policies concerning safety and accountability—at least on assault weapons—and ease their pressure on acquiescent politicians who fear N.R.A. disapproval at election time. We can't let the N.R.A.'s political blackmail prevent the banning of assault weapons—designed only to kill police officers and the people they defend.

EVALUATING THE AUTHOR'S ARGUMENTS:

In this viewpoint Jimmy Carter argues for an assault weapons ban, mentioning statistics on deaths attributable to the use of these weapons. Jacob Sullum, author of the following viewpoint, opposes such a ban. With which author do you tend to agree? Explain your reasoning, using evidence from the viewpoints.

Viewpoint

2

It Is Not Necessary to Reinstate the Federal Assault Weapon Ban

"The definition of 'assault weapons' has little to do with features that make a practical difference in the hands of criminals."

Jacob Sullum

In the following viewpoint Jacob Sullum argues that there is no reason to think that a reinstated ban on assault weapons will stop criminals. Sullum contends that there is confusion in the media about the difference between assault weapons and other guns. He claims that the definition of assault weapons is arbitrary as far as the tendency to inflict harm. Furthermore, Sullum argues that a ban on certain kinds of weapons will simply cause criminals to use other types of weapons for the same ends.

Sullum is a senior editor at *Reason* magazine and Reason.com and is a nationally syndicated columnist.

Jacob Sullum, "The Gunman and the Gun Ban," Reason.com, March 18, 2009. Copyright © 2009 by Reason Foundation, 3415 S. Sepulveda Blvd., Suite 400, Los Angeles, CA 90034, www.reason.com. Reproduced by permission.

AS YOU READ, CONSIDER THE FOLLOWING QUESTIONS:
1. According to Sullum, what is the difference between an assault
   rifle and the guns covered by assault weapons bans?
2. Why does the author claim that a ban on magazines holding
   more than ten rounds is not effective at deterring criminals like
   Michael McLendon?
3. The top two deadliest mass shootings in US history were accomplished using what type of weapon, according to Sullum?

Less than a day after Michael McLendon fired his last shot [on March 10, 2009], gun control groups issued press releases that cited his murderous rampage through three Alabama towns as an argument for reviving the federal "assault weapon" ban. The [Barack] Obama administration also wants to bring back the ban, on the theory that outlawing the firearms supposedly favored by gangbangers and homicidal maniacs will reduce the casualties they inflict. But there is little reason to believe such laws can deliver on that promise.

A Confusion About Gun Types

Last week [in early March 2009] Paul Helmke, president of the Brady Campaign to Prevent Gun Violence, claimed McLendon "needed the firepower of assault weapons to execute his plan of mass car-nage." In a joint statement, five anti-gun groups [Brady Campaign to Prevent Gun Violence, Coalition to Stop Gun Violence, Freedom States Alliance, Legal Community Against Violence, and Violence Policy Center] demanded "an effective federal assault weapons ban," calling the Alabama massacre the latest in "a string of preventable trag-edies committed with these military-style weapons." They identified McLendon's weapons as "a Bushmaster AR-15-style assault rifle and an SKS assault rifle," which they described as "military-bred firearms developed for the specific purpose of killing human beings quickly and efficiently."

In truth, neither of these guns is an assault rifle, which by defini-tion is capable of firing automatically. Both of McLendon's rifles, like all the guns covered by "assault weapon" bans, were semiautomatic, firing once per trigger pull.

Gun control groups deliberately foster confusion between "assault weapons," an arbitrary category based mainly on appearances, and machine guns, which are already strictly regulated under federal law. The confusion was apparent in news coverage of McLendon's shooting spree, which erroneously called his guns "automatic weapons" and "high powered assault rifles."

Michael McLendon (shown here in his high school graduation photo) went on a shooting spree in Alabama in 2009, killing eleven people, including himself. The incident added fuel to the debate on banning assault weapons.

The Definition of Assault Weapons

Furthermore, the standard version of the SKS, because it has a fixed magazine, was not covered by the federal "assault weapon" ban. It's not clear from press accounts whether McLendon's Bushmaster rifle would have been covered by the law; the company makes a "post-ban" version of the AR-15 that complies with state laws similar to the federal "assault weapon" ban because it does not have a collapsible stock or a bayonet mount.

As those modifications suggest, the definition of "assault weapons" has little to do with features that make a practical difference in the hands of criminals (who in any event rarely use these guns). The aspect of the federal "assault weapon" law that had the most functional significance was the ban on magazines holding more than 10 rounds. But that provision is unlikely to make a difference in crimes like McLendon's, since magazines can be switched in a few seconds and the time can be shortened by tapping them together (as McLendon did). Not to mention the fact that plenty of pre-ban large-capacity magazines would be available to a determined killer.

An Irrelevant Distinction Among Guns

In any case, the focus on the specific guns used in attacks like this is misleading because murderers don't need much "firepower" when they're attacking defenseless victims at random. The day after McLendon, using a rifle that anti-gun activists called an "assault weapon," killed 10 people in Alabama, a teenager used a 9mm Beretta pistol to kill 15 people in Germany. The deadliest mass shooting in U.S. history was accomplished with two ordinary handguns; so was the second deadliest.

McLendon carried a .38-caliber handgun and a shotgun in addition to his rifles, at least one of which apparently did not qualify as an "assault weapon." Had he been prevented from buying the

American Opinion Poll on an Assault Rifles Ban

When polled about whether they approved of legislation that would make the manufacturing, selling, and possession of assault rifles illegal, Americans gave the following responses:

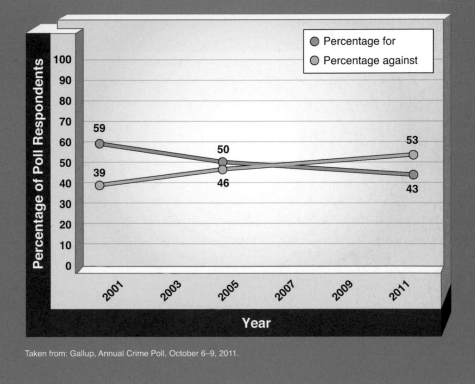

Taken from: Gallup, Annual Crime Poll, October 6–9, 2011.

Bushmaster, he could have armed himself with any number of hunting rifles that accept detachable magazines. As an agent with the federal Bureau of Alcohol, Tobacco, Firearms, and Explosives noted after the murders, "any gun is lethal."

Last year, when the U.S. Supreme Court [in *District of Columbia v. Heller* (2008)] explicitly recognized for the first time that the Second Amendment protects an individual right to arms, it suggested that prohibiting "dangerous and unusual weapons" nevertheless could be constitutional. That is the loophole supporters of "assault weapon" bans will try to exploit. Their success will depend on the extent to which the courts scrutinize the specious distinction between good and evil guns.

There Should Be a National Right-to-Carry Law

> *"[T]he Act recognizes that the Second Amendment guarantees the fundamental, individual right of every law-abiding citizen to bear arms for safety when traveling."*

Chris Cox

In the following viewpoint Chris Cox argues that H.R. 822, the National Right-to-Carry Reciprocity Act of 2011, is an important bill that should be made law. Cox says that the act would allow individuals who have concealed gun permits in their own states to carry their concealed guns in other states that allow such permits, without having to get an additional permit in that state. He concludes that such a law would be a good reform.

Cox is the executive director of the National Rifle Association's Institute for Legislative Action and serves as the organization's chief lobbyist.

AS YOU READ, CONSIDER THE FOLLOWING QUESTIONS:
1. According to Cox, the National Right-to-Carry Reciprocity Act of 2011 would allow anyone with a state-issued concealed firearm permit to do what?
2. The author contends that the current problem for permit holders is what?
3. What statistics does the author provide to support his argument that states with concealed carry permits are safer?

Thanks to the good work of millions of American gun owners and NRA members, Congress is moving closer to restoring one of our fundamental freedoms guaranteed by the Second Amendment.

Ten days ago, the House Judiciary Committee considered amendments to the "National Right-to-Carry-Reciprocity Act" (H.R. 822), which would allow any person with a valid, state-issued concealed firearm permit to exercise the right to carry a firearm in any state that permits concealed carry.

Some members of the Committee tried to weaken the bill with anti-gun amendments, and I'm happy to report that every one of them failed. The committee is expected to pass the bill soon, after which it will go before the full House for a vote.

As of today, 49 states have laws in place that permit their citizens to carry a concealed firearm in some form or another. Only Illinois completely denies its residents the right to carry a concealed firearm outside their homes or businesses for self-defense, an injustice for which President Obama fought hard when he was an Illinois state senator.

In 41 of these 49 states, law-abiding citizens can carry a firearm without having to navigate an overly restrictive bureaucratic process.

The problem is that some states allow visiting permit holders from other states to exercise their right to carry, and some states do not. As you can imagine, this presents a nightmare for interstate travel, as many Americans are forced to check their Second Amendment rights, and their fundamental right to self-defense, at the state line.

The National Right-to-Carry Reciprocity Act would solve this problem by simply requiring states that allow concealed carry to recognize each other's permits. Nothing more.

Predictably, gun-ban organizations like the Brady Campaign and New York City Mayor Michael Bloomberg's deceptively named "Mayors Against Illegal Guns" are doing everything they can to demonize H.R. 822, as are their allies in the anti-gun media.

Chris Cox (pictured), executive director of the National Rifle Association, supports the National Right-to-Carry Reciprocity Act of 2011 because it would allow individuals who have valid concealed gun permits to carry in any state that permits concealed carry.

First, they tried to scare Americans into thinking that H.R. 822 would unleash a new "wild west" atmosphere in the United States. This tactic fell flat because nearly every state in the nation already allows concealed carry and none of these outlandish predictions have materialized. In fact, quite the opposite has occurred.

On average, the 41 states that have the most tolerant right-to-carry laws have 22 percent lower total violent crime rates, 30 percent lower murder rates, 46 percent lower robbery rates and 12 percent lower aggravated assault rates, compared to the rest of the country. This is likely due to the fact that, as a group, citizens with permits to carry a firearm are more law-abiding than the general public.

Having failed at scaring Americans, the gun banners are now falling back on the Tenth Amendment [powers that are not granted to the federal government nor prohibited to the States by the Constitution are reserved to the States or the people] as their main argument against H.R. 822. It's a poorly conceived argument, as you might expect from groups that spend the majority of their time trying to trample the same "states' rights" that they now want to hold up as sacrosanct.

The fact is the Tenth Amendment is most certainly sacrosanct—that's why, in the 1990s, the NRA supported a successful constitutional challenge to provisions of the Brady [Handgun Violence Prevention] Act that violated it. But the National Right-to-Carry Reciprocity Act doesn't violate the Tenth Amendment. Rather, the Act recognizes that the Second Amendment guarantees the fundamental, individual right of every law-abiding citizen to bear arms for safety when traveling.

FAST FACT

H.R. 822, the National Right-to-Carry Reciprocity Act of 2011, passed in the US House of Representatives in November 2011 but as of March 2012 had not come up for a vote in the Senate.

This is an inalienable right that neither the federal government, nor any state government, may infringe upon. In addition, the Fourteenth Amendment gives Congress the power to protect us from states that infringe on our inalienable, constitutional rights.

House Vote on Passage: H.R. 822; National Right-to-Carry Reciprocity Act of 2011

Vote Overview, November 16, 2011*

Totals		Democrats	Republicans	Independents
Aye:	272	43	229	0
No:	154	147	7	0
Not Voting:	7	2	5	0
Required:	Simple majority of 426 votes (= 214 votes)			

*Vacancies in Congress will affect vote totals.

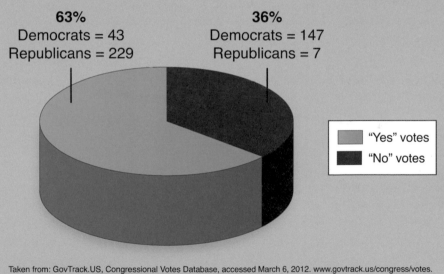

63%
Democrats = 43
Republicans = 229

36%
Democrats = 147
Republicans = 7

"Yes" votes
"No" votes

Taken from: GovTrack.US, Congressional Votes Database, accessed March 6, 2012. www.govtrack.us/congress/votes.

By the way, these are the same gun-ban groups that don't give any consideration to states' rights when they lobby for sweeping federal gun bans, ammunition bans, and magazine bans.

NRA has made the National Right-to-Carry Reciprocity Act a top priority because it restores a fundamental, inalienable right guaranteed to all law-abiding Americans by the Second Amendment. All Second

Amendment advocates, gun owners and pro-gun groups should be campaigning for the passage of this bill.

Also, as a general rule, no one should ever take seriously any lessons on constitutional law from groups whose sole mission is to destroy our most basic civil right guaranteed in the Constitution: the right to bear arms and defend ourselves and our loved ones, no matter which state we're in.

EVALUATING THE AUTHOR'S ARGUMENTS:

In this viewpoint Chris Cox claims that the National Right-to-Carry Reciprocity Act of 2011 should be passed. How might a proponent of states' rights dispute Cox's position?

Viewpoint

4

There Should Not Be a National Right-to-Carry Law

"The National Right-to-Carry Act effectively eliminates all state choice in the matter."

John Conyers Jr.

In the following viewpoint John Conyers Jr. argues that H.R. 822, the National Right-to-Carry Reciprocity Act of 2011, should not be passed. He claims that by allowing the concealed carry permit of one state to work in any other state that allows concealed weapons, the rights of states are violated. Conyers contends that the law will effectively allow concealed carry at the lowest common denominator and threaten public safety.

Conyers is a Democratic member of the US House of Representatives, representing Michigan since 1965.

AS YOU READ, CONSIDER THE FOLLOWING QUESTIONS:

1. According to Conyers, how many states will not grant concealed carry permits to people who have a record of alcohol abuse?
2. The author reports that which two places in the United States do not allow concealed carry?
3. Which three police organizations does Conyers claim oppose H.R. 822, the National Right-to-Carry Reciprocity Act of 2011?

Today [November 16, 2011], instead of working to create jobs, the Congress will consider the National Right-to-Carry Reciprocity Act, H.R. 822. This bill is special-interest legislation at its worst. It is opposed by virtually everyone with an interest in protecting public safety—law enforcement, policy experts, and state and local governments. But it will appease the National Rifle Association [N.R.A.], at least briefly, and so the Majority will bring it to the floor.

Different Laws in Different States

Under the National Right-to-Carry Reciprocity Act, a concealed firearm permit issued by any state would be valid in every state that allows concealed carry. If it passes, a visitor to my home state of Michigan would be allowed to carry a loaded, hidden weapon in public, even if he has not met the minimum requirements to do so mandated by our state law.

The fact is that different states have enacted different requirements for carrying a concealed weapon within their borders. Thirty-five states require applicants for a concealed carry license to complete some degree of firearms safety training. Twenty-nine states will not grant a permit to individuals with a record of alcohol abuse. Although federal law prohibits individuals with felony convictions from possessing a weapon, thirty-eight states have chosen to deny concealed carry licenses to individuals with convictions for certain misdemeanor offenses—such as stalking, sexual assault, and impersonating a police officer.

> **FAST FACT**
>
> Four states—Alaska, Arizona, Vermont, and Wyoming—allow residents to carry a concealed firearm without a permit.

Some states have voluntarily entered into reciprocity agreements with other states. Under current law, however, states may exit these agreements at any time. Such is the case in New Mexico and Nevada, which recently stopped recognizing Utah permits because Utah does not require live-fire instruction. Virginia will not honor permits from Alabama, Colorado, Georgia, Idaho, Indiana, Iowa, or New

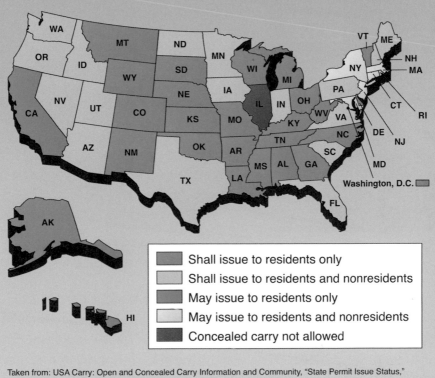

Concealed Carry Permit Issue Status, by State, March 2012

Legend:
- Shall issue to residents only
- Shall issue to residents and nonresidents
- May issue to residents only
- May issue to residents and nonresidents
- Concealed carry not allowed

Washington, D.C.

Taken from: USA Carry: Open and Concealed Carry Information and Community, "State Permit Issue Status," accessed March 6, 2012. www.usacarry.com

Hampshire because those states do not provide law enforcement with a reliable means to verify out-of-state permits. Idaho and Indiana choose to honor Virginia permits anyway.

A States' Rights Problem

The National Right-to-Carry Act effectively eliminates all state choice in the matter. State decisions about eligibility to carry a firearm in public will be stripped away in favor of the lowest common denominator.

The notion that the manager's amendment adopted by the Majority in the Judiciary Committee will solve this states' rights problem—by protecting jurisdictions that allow no concealed carry at all—is

US Representative John Conyers Jr. (pictured), the author of this viewpoint, opposed the National Right-to-Carry Reciprocity Act because he believes it violates states' rights.

fundamentally unserious. Presently, only Illinois and the District of Columbia fall into this exception. Given that the Majority offered an amendment in markup to impose this bill on the District of Columbia, the safety of its residents notwithstanding, we cannot expect even this "solution" to last long under H.R. 822.

The Majority argues that our Second Amendment rights, as articulated in *District of Columbia v. Heller* [2008] and other recent cases, ought to trump the concerns of state and local law enforcement when it comes to concealed weapons. *Heller* stands for no such thing. That case outlined a basic right to bear arms for the purpose of "self-defense in the home," but specifically recognized the constitutionality of state regulations on concealed weapons. We cannot allow the gun lobby to use *Heller* as a basis for discarding our state laws or our common sense.

A Threat to Public Safety

Worst of all, H.R. 822 is a direct threat to public safety. During a traffic stop, with a firearm in view, police officers must make split-second decisions for their own protection and the protection of others. But by forcing H.R. 822 on the states, the Majority also forces officers in that situation to contend with permits from forty-eight different jurisdictions—often with no means to verify their authenticity.

It is no wonder that this bill is opposed by organizations like the International Association of Chiefs of Police, the Major Cities Chiefs Association, and the Police Foundation. Reasonable minds can disagree about the conditions we ought to set on the possession of firearms, but we should not put officers at risk solely to appease the N.R.A.

Last week, voters across the country rejected conservative overreach on all fronts. Today, the Majority has an opportunity to heed that warning. With public safety at risk, and with so many more pressing issues before us, I urge my colleagues to reject this bill. [The bill passed the House, 272–154.]

EVALUATING THE AUTHOR'S ARGUMENTS:

In this viewpoint John Conyers Jr. argues that the National Right-to-Carry Reciprocity Act of 2011 violates the rights of states to have their own regulations. What other rights are competing with state rights on this issue?

Guns Should Be Allowed on College Campuses

C.J. Ciaramella

"Law-abiding students with concealed carry licenses are not asking for Wild West shootouts. They're asking for a right they've already been found responsible enough to exercise in public."

In the following viewpoint C.J. Ciaramella argues that handgun bans on college campuses should be lifted, allowing students who choose to carry weapons to exercise their right to do so. Ciaramella claims that the fight to lift the bans is making headway in the courts. He denies that the bans make college campuses safer, arguing instead that there is evidence that allowing guns on campus will increase safety by allowing students to act in self-defense when a campus shooting occurs.

Ciaramella is a writer for the *Daily Caller*, an online news and commentary publication.

AS YOU READ, CONSIDER THE FOLLOWING QUESTIONS:
1. According to Ciaramella, what state explicitly prohibits public colleges from banning licensed handguns on campus?
2. What US Supreme Court case does the author cite in support of his view that students should not be denied their rights in school?
3. Ciaramella cites a study claiming that the number of crimes per year at Colorado State University dropped by how many from 2003 to 2008, after licensed concealed carry was allowed in 2003?

A little more than three years ago [on April 16, 2007] Seung-Hui Cho entered a building at Virginia Tech, chained the doors shut and began shooting. He killed 32 people—the deadliest school shooting in United States history. The tragedy sparked a nationwide review of campus safety measures. Colleges began coordinating with local police to update old and outdated emergency policies. But the shooting also caused many students, dismayed by the poor emergency response by Virginia Tech administrators and police, to start looking toward ensuring their own safety. A movement was born to roll back long-standing handgun bans at colleges, led by the group Students for Concealed Carry on Campus [SCCC].

The Debate over Gun-Free Zones

The campaign argues that gun-free zones, far from ensuring the safety of students, leaves them defenseless. As David Burnett, the director of public relations for SCCC, said in a phone interview, "We find these pieces of paper tacked to the door that say 'no guns allowed' aren't doing much to deter shooters or even average criminals."

However, despite heavy media coverage and continued debate, advocates of concealed carry have little to show for their efforts. States have considered legislation to allow concealed carry on public campuses 34 times in the years since the Virginia Tech shooting, and more bills are expected this year. Yet so far, none of the legislation has passed in the face of heavy opposition from college administrators and faculty.

An opposing group, the Campaign to Keep Guns Off Campus, was started in 2008. In a phone interview, director Andy Pelosi (no relation to the [US] House [of Representatives] speaker [Nancy Pelosi]) said the campaign has collected the signatures of 133 colleges in 31 states which support handgun bans.

Currently [as of May 2010], 26 states ban handguns on campus, even by those with concealed carry permits. Twenty-three other states leave the decision to individual colleges. Only Utah explicitly prohibits public colleges from banning licensed handguns on campus.

Handgun Bans in the Courts

But concealed carry advocates have fared better in the courts. A Colorado appellate court recently struck down Colorado University's ban on handguns, ruling it conflicted with the state constitution.

A handgun ban on Oregon public campuses is also currently under review by the state supreme court. Filed by the Oregon Firearms Federation, the lawsuit seeks clarification, similar to the Colorado case, on whether the Oregon University System has the power to regulate handguns.

Oregon law allows licensed citizens to carry a concealed handgun in almost any public building in the state. It also grants the legislative assembly sole power to regulate firearms. However, the Oregon University System maintains an absolute ban on weapons.

The case was spurred by the ordeal of Jeffrey Maxwell, a Western Oregon University [WOU] student and Marine veteran. Maxwell was arrested in January 2009 for possessing a concealed handgun on campus, even though he was licensed to carry.

The county D.A. [district attorney] released Maxwell after determining he had not broken any laws. Nevertheless, he was still sus-

FAST FACT

On March 5, 2012, the Colorado Supreme Court struck down the University of Colorado's campus gun ban that blocked students and employees from carrying licensed concealed weapons, finding that the state's Concealed Carry Act protects students' rights.

A college student displays his handgun. Opponents of campus gun bans say there is growing evidence that such bans do not make college campuses safer but that allowing guns on campus does provide a safer environment.

pended from WOU and ordered by a tribunal of fellow students to undergo a psychiatric evaluation. After a long legal battle, WOU eventually dropped all disciplinary actions against Maxwell.

Cases like these probably offer the best chance for proponents of concealed carry to defeat campus bans, but even in states where there is no such legal conflict, is there a justification for banning guns from campuses? If a student is licensed by the state to carry, what is the fundamental difference between a classroom and any other public space?

"It makes no sense," Oregon Firearms Federation Executive Director Kevin Starrett said in a phone intervew. "If we can't trust them on campus, why do we trust them anywhere else?"

Indeed, if students' First Amendment right to free expression does not end at the school gates, as the Supreme Court ruled in *Tinker v. Des Moines*, [1969] why should they be denied their Second Amendment right to self-defense?

Concealed Carry Laws on College Campuses, by State, December 2011

Twenty-two states ban carrying a concealed weapon on college campuses. In twenty-five states, colleges and universities decide individually whether or not to allow concealed carry weapons on their campuses.

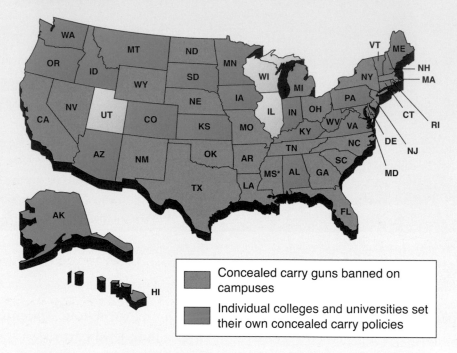

Concealed carry guns banned on campuses

Individual colleges and universities set their own concealed carry policies

*According to a 2011 law, Mississippi allows concealed carry for those who have taken a voluntary firearms safety course, but the law is being disputed.

Taken from: National Conference of State Legislatures, "Guns on Campus: Overview," December 2–11. www.ncsl.org.

Guns and Safety

Opponents of guns on campus argue that colleges are already safe and introducing guns would only make them more dangerous.

"The studies that we refer to show that campuses are very safe environments for the most part," Pelosi said. "At this point, we don't see the need for introducing guns on campus. If you introduce guns, you are asking for bad outcomes."

Pelosi said college campuses, with their volatile mix of alcohol, crowded dorms and flaring emotions, are no place for guns. Plus, he said, school shootings were exceedingly uncommon: "These types of instances are so rare, the positives just don't outweigh the negatives."

However, Burnett called that argument "cold comfort" for the victims of college shootings. "Just because the crime rate might be a little lower on campuses doesn't erase the need for self-defense," Burnett said. "If there is one shooting on college campuses a year—just one— the students should have that right to self-defense."

And even if shootings are relatively rare, students have other things to worry about, especially female students. A 2009 study by the Center for Public Integrity reported that up to 20 percent of college women will be sexually assaulted before they graduate. College neighborhoods are also hot spots for burglaries and muggings.

In light of this, a compelling argument can also be made that guns makes campuses *more* safe. According to campus police statistics culled by SCCC, the number of crimes per year at Colorado State University, where licensed concealed carry has been allowed since 2003, has dropped from a high of more than 800 in 2002 to less than 300 in 2008.

At Colorado University, where handguns are still banned for the moment, Burnett said, crime has only risen.

Law-abiding students with concealed carry licenses are not asking for Wild West shootouts. They're asking for a right they've already been found responsible enough to exercise in public. They're asking— because nowhere is perfectly safe—for at least a fighting chance.

EVALUATING THE AUTHOR'S ARGUMENTS:

In this viewpoint C.J. Ciaramella argues that students should be allowed to carry weapons, in part for their own safety. How might Alex Hannaford, author of the following viewpoint, dispute that line of reasoning?

Viewpoint
6

Guns Should Not Be Allowed on College Campuses

"Guns are designed for one thing only—and the more of them there are, the greater the chance of someone getting hurt."

Alex Hannaford

In the following viewpoint Alex Hannaford argues that laws to allow concealed weapons on college campuses are misguided. Hannaford claims that although several recent attempts by states to pass campus-carry legislation have failed, the gun rights lobby is powerful and persistent and will continue to push state legislation. Hannaford contends that guns are a particularly bad idea at colleges, where alcohol is ubiquitous and hormones run rampant.

Hannaford is a British journalist based in Texas.

AS YOU READ, CONSIDER THE FOLLOWING QUESTIONS:

1. In which two states does Hannaford report that legislation to allow concealed weapons on campus recently failed?
2. What pro–gun rights organization has called President Barack Obama a "committed anti-gunner," according to the author?
3. According to research cited by the author, people in favor of concealed weapons see what two major threats as operative?

Alex Hannaford, "The Campus Carry Movement Stutter-Steps Across America," *Atlantic*, May 10, 2011. Reproduced by permission of the author.

L ast October [2010], an email popped into my inbox from Mike Stollenwerk, co-founder of gun rights networking hub OpenCarry.org, which boasts the motto, "A right un-exercised is a right lost." He was responding to a question I had about the possible re-tabling of a bill in the Texas legislature which would, if passed, allow students to carry handguns with them to college.

The Push for Campus-Carry Legislation

At the time, only Utah allowed the carrying of concealed weapons into the classrooms of public universities, while Colorado left it up to the colleges themselves to decide. Stollenwerk wrote: "My bet is that there are a fair number of college students and faculty members across America who, after the Virginia Tech murders, have decided to regularly carry loaded concealed handguns to class even when it violates college administrative rules. . . . I hope campus carry is legalized in Texas soon."

But faculty members weren't as keen on their students packing heat during their lessons as Stollenwerk thought they might be. Last month [April 2011], just as state senators were ready to send a bill to allow handguns on campus to a final vote, University of Texas (UT) Chancellor Francisco Cigarroa wrote a public letter to legislators saying the gun bill was a bad idea. And he had the public support of both the UT Faculty Counsel and Texas A&M University Faculty Senate. The result: the bill stalled in the Texas senate, lacking the two-thirds of votes needed to get it on to the floor.

But Sen. Jeff Wentworth, the Texas Republican who authored the bill, was persistent, and yesterday [May 9, 2011] he managed to get it tacked on to a piece of education finance reform legislation which passed the state senate.

If the bill in Texas becomes law, some professors there have said they plan to include a clause in syllabi stipulating that students are not be permitted to carry guns into their classroom—and then simply refuse to teach classes where students don't assent.

Campus-carry legislation was also on the move this spring in Arizona. Three weeks ago, the state's conservative governor Jan Brewer vetoed a gun rights bill that had already made its way successfully through both houses, saying it was "poorly written" and that allowing

Republican state senator Jeff Wentworth of Texas (pictured) pushed a bill through the state legislature that would allow Texas college students to carry concealed guns on campus, despite opposition from the University of Texas and Texas A&M University.

guns to be carried in "public rights of way" could have included K–12 schools—something prohibited under state and federal law.

But the hiccup in Arizona hasn't stopped the movement to allow guns on campus gather momentum elsewhere. This year alone an astonishing 20 states have seen "guns on campus" bills introduced (so far seven have failed).

The Power of the Gun Rights Lobby

The non-profit Brady Campaign to Prevent Gun Violence points out that since the 2007 Virginia Tech massacre, campus-carry legislation has been stymied 51 times in 27 states. But they shouldn't sit back and breathe a sigh of relief just yet. In Arizona, Brewer has signaled that she'd consider future campus-carry legislation if it addressed her concerns.

The gun rights lobby is powerful—and persistent. And here's a peculiar anomaly: that movement seems emboldened by the perception that President [Barack] Obama is a "committed anti-gunner," as the Gun Owners of America organization said during his initial run for president. This perception persists despite the fact that the Brady Campaign issued a report card last year failing him on all of the issues it considered important—including closing gun show loopholes and curbing trafficking.

In fact, since taking office, Obama has signed a law permitting guns to be taken into national parks and wildlife refuges and another allowing people to check guns as baggage on Amtrak. During a campaign speech in Virginia back in 2008 he declared: "I will not take your shotgun away. I will not take your rifle away. I won't take your handgun away." If anything, until now the Obama administration's hands-off attitude toward gun control has paved the way for the campus-carry movement to flourish, while the misperception that he wants to take people's guns away has been used as an effective tool to bolster support for Second Amendment groups.

The Brady Campaign's Brian Malte told me that since his organization issued Obama an "F" on his report card for his first year in office, the president has made some steps in the right direction: a few weeks ago he wrote an op-ed piece for the *Arizona Star* newspaper in which he emphasized the need for failsafe background checks for gun owners. "An unbalanced man shouldn't be able to buy a gun so easily," he wrote. And he nominated Andrew Traver to head up the Bureau of Alcohol, Tobacco, Firearms and Explosives—a man who has been outspoken on gangs and weapon control, and whose nomination the NRA [National Rifle Association] opposes.

FAST FACT

In January 2012, Senate Bill 1474 was introduced in the Arizona legislature. The law would allow anyone twenty-one or older with a concealed-carry permit to bring a firearm on campus.

College Students and Guns

But none of this is likely to have any effect on the lobby to push campus-carry legislation at the state level. And I don't like the idea of anyone carrying a gun in public, let alone a 21-year-old student fueled by testosterone and alcohol. When I was at university in the mid-'90s,

Violent Crimes on Campus and Nationwide, 2008

Crime	College Campuses	Nationwide	% of National
Murder*	16	16,272	0.10%
Robbery	1,959	441,855	0.44%
Aggravated Assault	2,717	834,885	0.33%

*Includes nonnegligent manslaughter only

Taken from: Center for Higher Education Policy, December 6, 2010. www.popecenter.org. Data sources: FBI Uniform Crime Report and Department of Education Statistics.

we drank far more than was good for us. Add guns to the mix and it's a volatile concoction. When you think of it like that: giving guns to young students largely interested in sex and booze, I'd wager it seems less of a genius idea.

Angela Stroud, a PhD candidate at the University of Texas, has spent the last two years researching the social meanings of concealed handgun licensing. She's conducted over 40 interviews and even took the handgun license test herself so she'd be more informed. She told me there are those opposed to guns who consider "what's best for society," and those who are pro–second amendment for whom the "greater good" does not form part of their argument. "There is a major privileging of the individual," she said. "And it's a powerful experience to become enmeshed in this worldview. There's a fear. Instead of saying that incidents like Virginia Tech rarely happen, they say that even a one-in-a-million chance of being murdered is a frightening thing. They see two major threats—one is a criminal who wants to kill you; the other is a government that wants to control you."

For me, the argument that you could prevent another Virginia Tech with more guns is fatuous. Guns are designed for one thing only—and the more of them there are, the greater the chance of someone getting hurt. Texas Senator Rodney Ellis issued a statement saying the bill would do nothing to improve the safety of students on campus in his state and could, in fact, make dangerous situations more deadly by creating confusion for law enforcement. "We don't need to incentivize campus Rambos," he said.

I couldn't agree more.

EVALUATING THE AUTHOR'S ARGUMENTS:

In this viewpoint Alex Hannaford contends that college students' interests in sex and alcohol makes them poor candidates for carrying concealed weapons. How might a person who opposed Hannaford's view claim that this line of reasoning leads to a reductio ad absurdum (the carrying of something to an absurd extreme) fallacy in which no one is a good candidate for carrying weapons?

Chapter 3

What Measures Should Be Taken to Reduce Gun Violence?

Illegal handguns confiscated by Philadelphia police are displayed here. Police associations across the country have advocated measures that would get such guns off the streets. They have been met with opposition by the National Rifle Association.

Stricter Gun Regulations Are Needed to Reduce Gun Violence

"We need to make it harder for convicted felons, the dangerously mentally ill, and other prohibited persons to obtain guns by implementing strong gun laws and policies."

Brady Campaign to Prevent Gun Violence

In the following viewpoint the Brady Campaign to Prevent Gun Violence contends that there are high numbers of victims of gun violence in the United States because it is too easy to get a gun. The campaign claims that guns do not make people safer and that having more guns simply leads to more deaths. The Brady Campaign contends that stricter regulations will lead to fewer guns in the hands of those who will misuse them and, thus, less gun violence.

The Brady Campaign to Prevent Gun Violence works to pass and enforce sensible federal and state gun laws, regulations, and public policies.

AS YOU READ, CONSIDER THE FOLLOWING QUESTIONS:
1. According to the Brady Campaign, over how many people have been killed with guns in the United States since 1968?
2. As reported in the viewpoint, keeping a firearm in the home increases the risk of homicide by what factor?
3. According to the author, what percentage of gun acquisitions happen on the secondary market, without a background check?

There are too many victims of gun violence because we make it too easy for dangerous people to get dangerous weapons in America.

Gun Deaths in the United States

DID YOU KNOW? In one year on average, almost 100,000 people in America are shot or killed with a gun.

In one year, 31,593 people died from gun violence and 66,769 people survived gun injuries. That includes:
- 12,179 people murdered and 44,466 people shot in an attack.
- 18,223 people who killed themselves and 3,031 people who survived a suicide attempt with a gun.
- 592 people who were killed unintentionally and 18,610 who were shot unintentionally but survived.

Over a million people have been killed with guns in the United States since 1968, when Dr. Martin Luther King, Jr. and Robert F. Kennedy were assassinated.

U.S. homicide rates are 6.9 times higher than rates in 22 other populous high-income countries combined, despite similar non-lethal crime and violence rates. The firearm homicide rate in the U.S. is 19.5 times higher.

Among 23 populous, high-income countries, 80 percent of all firearm deaths occurred in the United States.

Gun violence impacts society in countless ways: medical costs, costs of the criminal justice system, security precautions such as metal detectors, and reductions in quality of life because of fear of gun violence. These impacts are estimated to cost U.S. citizens $100 billion annually.

The Prevalence of Guns

DID YOU KNOW? Where there are more guns, there are more gun deaths.

An estimated 41 percent of gun-related homicides and 94 percent of gun-related suicides would not [have occurred] under the same circumstances had no guns been present.

Higher household gun ownership correlates with higher rates of homicides, suicides, and unintentional shootings.

Keeping a firearm in the home increases the risk of suicide by a factor of 3 to 5 and increases the risk of suicide with a firearm by a factor of 17.

Cartoon by Signe Wilkinson's Editorial Cartoons, Cartoonist Group. Copyright © by Signe Wilkinson. All rights reserved. Reproduced by permission.

Keeping a firearm in the home increases the risk of homicide by a factor of 3.

DID YOU KNOW? On the whole, guns are more likely to raise the risk of injury than to confer protection.

A gun in the home is 22 times more likely to be used in a completed or attempted suicide (11x), criminal assault or homicide (7x), or unintentional shooting death or injury (4x) than to be used in a self-defense shooting.

Guns are used to intimidate and threaten 4 to 6 times more often than they are used to thwart crime.

FAST FACT

According to the Federal Bureau of Investigation, 68 percent of homicides in 2010 were committed with guns.

Every year there are only about 200 legally justified self-defense homicides by private citizens (FBI, Expanded Homicide Data, Table 15) compared with over 30,000 gun deaths.

A 2009 study found that people in possession of a gun are 4.5 times more likely to be shot in an assault.

The Need for Stronger Gun Laws

DID YOU KNOW? Assaults and suicide attempts with firearms are much more likely to be fatal than those perpetrated with less lethal weapons or means. Removing guns saves lives.

There are five times as many deaths from gun assaults as from knife assaults, where the rates of assault with knives and with guns are similar.

More than 90 percent of suicide attempts with a gun are fatal. In comparison, only 3 percent of attempts with drugs or cutting are fatal.

Paul Helmke (pictured), president of the Brady Center to Prevent Gun Violence, talks to reporters about gun violence and the fact that it is too easy for criminals to obtain illegal guns in the United States.

DID YOU KNOW? Guns can be sold in the United States without a background check to screen out criminals or the mentally ill.

It is estimated that over 40 percent of gun acquisitions occur in the secondary market. That means that they happen without a Brady background check at a federally licensed dealer.

Sales from federal firearm licensees (FFLs) require a background check. Sales between individuals, under federal law, do not require a background check. This means that felons can "lie and buy" at gun shows and other places where guns are readily available.

We need to make it harder for convicted felons, the dangerously mentally ill, and other prohibited persons to obtain guns by implementing strong gun laws and policies that will protect our families and communities from gun violence.

EVALUATING THE AUTHOR'S ARGUMENTS:

In this viewpoint the Brady Campaign to Prevent Gun Violence claims that stronger gun laws and polices will help to reduce gun violence by felons, the mentally ill, and other persons. What assumption is being made with which Charles C.W. Cooke, author of the following viewpoint, would disagree?

Viewpoint 2

Stricter Gun Regulations Will Not Reduce Gun Violence

"Those who are willing to break the laws against murder do not care about the regulation of firearms, and will get hold of weapons whether doing so is legal or not."

Charles C.W. Cooke

In the following viewpoint Charles C.W. Cooke argues that strengthening gun laws will not keep tragedies caused by gun violence from occurring. Using the example of the 2011 Norway attacks, Cooke claims that Norway's stringent gun laws not only did not stop the shooter but prevented him from being stopped sooner by another citizen or law enforcement officer. Cooke concludes that it is better to have more permissive gun laws for protection, since laws will not keep guns out of the hands of criminals.

Cooke is an editorial intern for the *National Review*, a conservative weekly magazine of news and commentary.

Charles C.W. Cooke, "Norway and Gun Control: Gun Laws Do Not Hit Their Target," *National Review* Online, July 27, 2011. www.nationalreview.com. Copyright © 2011 by National Review, Inc., 215 Lexington Avenue, New York, NY 10016. All rights reserved. Reproduced by permission.

AS YOU READ, CONSIDER THE FOLLOWING QUESTIONS:
1. What historical figure does Cooke quote in order to support his view that laws will not disarm criminals?
2. Rather than focus on where the Norwegian gunman was able to get his weapons, Cooke suggests that what issue be considered?
3. What example does the author give to support his view that the more permissive gun laws of the United States limit the damage of criminals?

Whenever a tragedy such as last week's attack [July 22, 2011] in Norway occurs, the first instinct of many is to ask how the perpetrator was able to get hold of a gun, and shortly after to conclude that Something Must Be Done About Guns. Among those to speak out after Friday's horror was Dennis Hennigan, president of the Brady Campaign to Prevent Gun Violence. Mr. Hennigan suggested that "such a tragedy in Norway likely will lead to determined efforts to further examine their nation's gun policies."

Laws and Criminals

Whether it will or not remains to be seen, but history shows us that this would be the wrong response. Those who are willing to break the laws against murder do not care about the regulation of firearms, and will get hold of weapons whether doing so is legal or not. As the old trope goes, to expect a mass-murderer to be concerned that his firearm is obtained outside the law is akin to expecting a truck bomber to fret that his vehicle is occupying two parking spaces.

Put simply, gun laws do not hit their target.

Norway already has strict regulation of firearms, but this is an irrelevance when considering the actions of Anders Breivik. There are also laws in that country

> **FAST FACT**
>
> Anders Behring Breivik was charged with two terrorist attacks that occurred in Norway on July 22, 2011, which killed 77 people and injured 151 others with a car bomb and two guns.

against impersonating a police officer, against setting off bombs, and against massacring children. Most people follow these. But then, most people are not the problem. Most people do not get out of bed and plan terrorist attacks. Those who do are beyond the law and will not be constrained by changes to it. In a free society, maniacs will always find a way.

Largest Civilian Firearms Arsenals, Ranked by Country

Country	Average Firearms per 100 People	Rank by Rate of Civilian Ownership
Northern Ireland	21.9	25
UAE	22.1	24
Greece	22.5	23
New Zealand	22.6	22
Montenegro	23.1	21
Macedonia	24.1	20
Kuwait	24.8	19
Bahrain	24.8	18
Oman	25.4	17
Germany	30.3	16
Iceland	30.3	15
Austria	30.4	14
Canada	30.8	13
France	31.2	12
Norway	31.3	11
Sweden	31.6	10
Uruguay	31.8	9
Iraq	34.2	8
Saudi Arabia	35	7
Cyprus	36.4	6
Serbia	37.8	5
Finland	45.3	4
Switzerland	45.7	3
Yemen	54.8	2
United States of America	88.8	1

Taken from: Graduate Institute of International Studies, *Small Arms Survey 2007: Guns and the City.* New York: Cambridge University Press, 2007.

This is not a new concept. [Italian politician] Cesare Beccaria out-lined this truth in his seminal book *Crimes & Punishments* in 1764, in a passage that made such an impression upon Thomas Jefferson that he copied it into his daybook and quoted it at length in letters to his nephew and to James Madison:

> The laws of this nature are those which forbid to wear arms, disarming those only who are not disposed to commit the crime which the laws mean to prevent. Can it be supposed, that those who have the courage to violate the most sacred laws of human-ity, and the most important of the code, will respect the less considerable and arbitrary injunctions, the violation of which is so easy, and of so little comparative importance? Does not the execution of this law deprive the subject of that personal liberty, so dear to mankind and to the wise legislator? And does it not subject the innocent to all the disagreeable circumstances that should only fall on the guilty? It certainly makes the situation of the assaulted worse and of the assailants better, and rather encourages than prevents murder, as it requires less courage to attack unarmed than armed persons.

Gun Laws in Norway

There are few laws that Norway could have passed to prevent such an attack. The fertilizer that Breivik used in his bomb was legally bought through a farm he had registered, and the guns he used in his rampage were legally registered. Guns are allowed in Norway only for hunting and sports shooting, with handgun licenses requiring the applicant to take a nine-hour firearm-safety course, pass a writ-ten test, and prove active and continuing membership of a shoot-ing club. This Breivik did, pointing explicitly in his application to his clean criminal record. Had he not been able to get hold of the weapons domestically, he would have found them elsewhere. (He had already taken an abortive trip to Prague with this aim, hollowing out the back seats of his car to make space for the AK-47 assault rifle and Glock pistol he coveted. He failed to make any connections with the many illicit weapons dealers for which Prague is famous, but that he was prepared to risk dying at the hands of what he described as

Even though Norway has strict firearms regulations, Anders Breivik (in red) was still able to procure deadly weapons. Using two guns and a car bomb, he killed seventy-seven people and wounded nearly twice that number.

"brutal and cynical criminals" to obtain firearms is an indication that he was unlikely to give up.)

A better question than "How did the shooter get his guns?" is "What would have happened had others at Utøya had had access to weapons too?" If Breivik had been denied his monopoly on violence, we may have read a different story. As it was, Breivik could have been fairly confident that he would not be challenged—even by the police, who are unarmed except in special circumstances, and who took an hour and a half to get to the scene.

Norway's system is the worst of both worlds. Licenses are tied to interests—farming, hunting, sports—rather than to rights. Transportation of firearms is heavily restricted, and there is no such thing as a concealed-carry permit. The police are unarmed. We have heard much about how "uncontroversial" the issue is in Norway, but it should be more so. Currently, it is a veritable paradise for those with ill intent who know that their actions will go unchecked.

Gun Laws in the United States

The United States is no stranger to gun violence, but it is inconceivable that a shooter could have terrorized such a large area for an hour and a half with impunity in, say, Idaho. When Charles Whitman ran amok at the University of Texas in 1966, his intended victims started shooting back. He was eventually killed by a policeman. As John Lott Jr. has persuasively argued, the relationship between guns and crime is counterintuitive; even those who do not own guns are protected by those who do, both actively and, because criminal behavior is affected by calculation of risk, passively.

To live in freedom is to expose ourselves to the occasional outburst of the insane and the criminal. We cannot stop those who have evil in their hearts, but we can make sure that those who do not—the citizenry and the police—are given a fighting chance to protect us all.

EVALUATING THE AUTHOR'S ARGUMENTS:

In this viewpoint Charles C.W. Cooke claims that unarmed citizens and police are more vulnerable to armed criminals. What kind of statistical information about Norway and the United States would support his view?

Viewpoint

3

Restrictions on Gun Sales Need to Be Strengthened

Barack Obama

"Our focus right now should be on sound and effective steps that will actually keep those irresponsible, law-breaking few from getting their hands on a gun in the first place."

In the following viewpoint Barack Obama argues that in the aftermath of the tragic shooting in Tucson, Arizona, which included the killing of a judge and the serious wounding of a US congresswoman—by a man known to be unstable—more needs to be done to keep guns out of the hands of the wrong people. Obama claims that the system for background checks is not being adequately utilized and that additional safeguards need to be implemented in order to ensure that gun sellers are selling guns only to responsible, law-abiding citizens.

Obama is the forty-fourth president of the United States.

AS YOU READ, CONSIDER THE FOLLOWING QUESTIONS:
1. How many people were killed or wounded in the Tucson, Arizona, shooting on January 8, 2011, according to Obama?
2. What filter does the author claim had not been adequately implemented to stop the wrong people from getting guns?
3. What two examples of extreme reaction to gun control reforms does Obama give?

It's been more than two months since the tragedy in Tucson [on January 8, 2011] stunned the nation. It was a moment when we came together as one people to mourn and to pray for those we lost. And in the attack's turbulent wake, Americans by and large rightly refrained from finger-pointing, assigning blame or playing politics with other people's pain.

The Impact of Gun Violence

But one clear and terrible fact remains. A man our Army rejected as unfit for service; a man one of our colleges deemed too unstable for studies; a man apparently bent on violence, was able to walk into a store and buy a gun. He used it to murder six people and wound 13 others. And if not for the heroism of bystanders and a brilliant surgical team, it would have been far worse.

But since that day, we have lost perhaps another 2,000 members of our American family to gun violence. Thousands more have been wounded. We lose the same number of young people to guns every day and a half as we did at Columbine, and every four days as we did at Virginia Tech. Every single day, America is robbed of more futures. It has awful consequences for our society. And as a society, we have a responsibility to do everything we can to put a stop to it.

The Politics of Guns

Now, like the majority of Americans, I believe that the Second Amendment guarantees an individual right to bear arms. And the courts have settled that as the law of the land. In this country, we have a strong tradition of gun ownership that's handed from generation to generation. Hunting and shooting are part of our national heritage.

And, in fact, my administration has not curtailed the rights of gun owners—it has expanded them, including allowing people to carry their guns in national parks and wildlife refuges.

The fact is, almost all gun owners in America are highly responsible. They're our friends and neighbors. They buy their guns legally and use them safely, whether for hunting or target shooting, collection or protection. And that's something that gun-safety advocates need to accept. Likewise, advocates for gun owners should accept the awful reality that gun violence affects Americans everywhere, whether on the streets of Chicago or at a supermarket in Tucson.

I know that every time we try to talk about guns, it can reinforce stark divides. People shout at one another, which makes it impossible to listen. We mire ourselves in stalemate, which makes it impossible to get to where we need to go as a country. However, I believe that if common sense prevails, we can get beyond wedge issues and stale

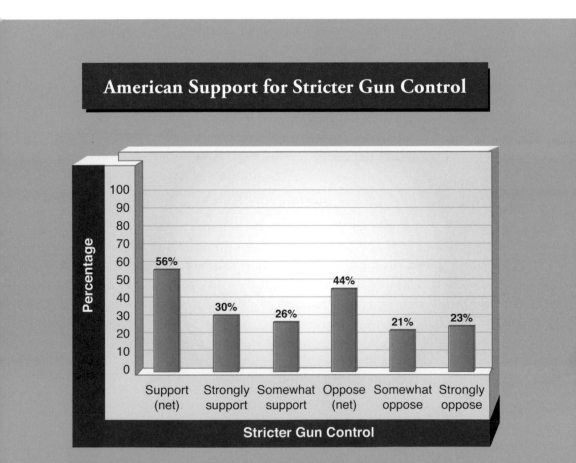

American Support for Stricter Gun Control

Note: Percentages may not add up to 100% due to rounding.

Taken from: Harris Interactive Poll, Poll #104, October 4, 2011. www.harrisinteractive.com.

political debates to find a sensible, intelligent way to make the United States of America a safer, stronger place.

Steps Toward Responsible Gun Sales

I'm willing to bet that responsible, law-abiding gun owners agree that we should be able to keep an irresponsible, law-breaking few—dangerous criminals and fugitives, for example—from getting their hands on a gun in the first place.

I'm willing to bet they don't think that using a gun and using common sense are incompatible ideas—that we should check someone's criminal record before he can check out at a gun seller; that an unbalanced man shouldn't be able to buy a gun so easily; that there's room for us to have reasonable laws that uphold liberty, ensure citizen safety and are fully compatible with a robust Second Amendment.

That's why our focus right now should be on sound and effective steps that will actually keep those irresponsible, law-breaking few from getting their hands on a gun in the first place.

- First, we should begin by enforcing laws that are already on the books. The National Instant Criminal Background Check System is the filter that's supposed to stop the wrong people from getting their hands on a gun. Bipartisan legislation four years ago [in 2007] was supposed to strengthen this system, but it hasn't been properly implemented. It relies on data supplied by states—but that data is often incomplete and inadequate. We must do better.
- Second, we should in fact reward the states that provide the best data—and therefore do the most to protect our citizens.
- Third, we should make the system faster and nimbler. We should provide an instant, accurate, comprehensive and consistent system for background checks to sellers who want to do the right thing, and make sure that criminals can't escape it.

President Barack Obama (pictured) believes that in order to keep guns out of the hands of the wrong people, additional safeguards must be implemented to ensure that gun sellers make sales only to responsible, law-abiding individuals.

Porous background checks are bad for police officers, for law-abiding citizens and for the sellers themselves. If we're serious about keeping guns away from someone who's made up his mind to kill, then we can't allow a situation where a responsible seller denies him a weapon at one store, but he effortlessly buys the same gun someplace else.

The Need for Consensus

Clearly, there's more we can do to prevent gun violence. But I want this to at least be the beginning of a new discussion on how we can keep America safe for all our people.

I know some aren't interested in participating. Some will say that anything short of the most sweeping anti-gun legislation is a capitulation to the gun lobby. Others will predictably cast any discussion as the opening salvo in a wild-eyed scheme to take away everybody's guns. And such hyperbole will become the fodder for overheated fundraising letters.

But I have more faith in the American people than that. Most gun-control advocates know that most gun owners are responsible citizens. Most gun owners know that the word "common sense" isn't a code word for "confiscation." And none of us should be willing to remain passive in the face of violence or resigned to watching helplessly as another rampage unfolds on television.

As long as those whose lives are shattered by gun violence don't get to look away and move on, neither can we. We owe the victims of the tragedy in Tucson and the countless unheralded tragedies each year nothing less than our best efforts—to seek consensus, to prevent future bloodshed, to forge a nation worthy of our children's futures.

EVALUATING THE AUTHOR'S ARGUMENTS:

In this viewpoint Barack Obama suggests that most people will find his suggestions to be justified by common sense. Do you think that Mike Piccione, author of the following viewpoint, would agree? Why or why not?

Viewpoint

4

Restrictions on Gun Sales Do Not Need to Be Strengthened

"More bureaucracy on law-abiding citizens is the easiest form of gun control and hidden under the label of 'common sense gun measures.'"

Mike Piccione

In the following viewpoint Mike Piccione argues that the push for legislation to restrict the sale of guns at gun shows is misguided. Piccione contends that the attempt to further restrict gun sales is part of the agenda of liberal legislators to increase bureaucracy and thereby stop citizens from owning guns. Piccione claims that restrictive gun control leads to greater crime, not to a safer society.

Piccione is founding editor of *Guns & Patriots* (a pro-gun weekly newsletter) and an executive at the US Concealed Carry Association.

AS YOU READ, CONSIDER THE FOLLOWING QUESTIONS:

1. What kind of license must a licensed gun dealer have, according to the author?
2. According to Piccione, closing the "gun show loophole" would allow the government to do what?
3. Why has New York City not eliminated crimes committed with guns, according to the author?

Mike Piccione, "Why Liberals Want Gun Shows Stopped," *Human Events,* March 15, 2011. Copyright © 2011 Human Events Inc. All rights reserved. Reproduced by permission.

A fundamental principle of a free people is the ability to transfer property to someone else without government intervention. In the case of firearms, it is often a tradition to pass on a gun from one generation to another.

The Push for More Restrictions

Recently a group called Mayors Against Illegal Guns, co-chaired by New York City Mayor Michael Bloomberg, commissioned a poll to determine how the public felt about tightening background checks on people that bought guns. It will come as little surprise that a group called Mayors Against Illegal Guns wants additional restrictive legislation on the already restrictive process and they even bought the research that indicates the public agrees.

The target of liberal legislators is the gun show. If you are a licensed gun dealer you hold a Federal Firearms License and are required by law to perform a background check before you can release the gun to the buyer. That makes good sense and often there is a waiting period. A waiting period makes good sense too unless you are someone being threatened or harassed and you happen to need a way to defend yourself. The attacker will be reassured that the government will deny you,

Countless guns are purchased at gun shows like this one, at which each seller must hold a federal firearms license. The author contends that the government is bent on increasing restrictions on private gun sales between individuals, since private sellers are currently not required to be licensed.

the potential victim, an immediate opportunity to purchase a tool to defend yourself. When an attack is going to happen in seconds the police, if called, will respond in minutes to take the crime report.

Here is the controversial aspect of a gun show: the unlicensed seller. This is a person that wants to sell his personal property to another individual. It is the equivalent of you saying "Mike, you want to sell that .22?" And then me telling you I'll take 50-bucks for it. We have a deal and I'm the unlicensed seller. But, I don't need a license to sell you my .22. That is the "gun show loophole."

A Means of Gun Control

Closing the "gun show loophole" enables the government to curtail person to person sales. That is what is really behind the attack on gun shows. Every gun would have to be turned into a gun dealer so that it could be tracked by the Federal Government and then the transfer process would be monitored by the Federal Government. The right you have now to sell your neighbor your shotgun will be gone, forever.

What is even more disturbing is the loss of the right to pass on your gun to a family member. The tradition of passing on grandpa's gun to his grandson will be legislated out of existence. Gramps will have to pass the gun to a federally authorized entity that will then register it and pass it on to the recipient. Often the gifting of the first firearm is to someone thirteen or fourteen years old. Because they can not legally own a gun at that age it would have to be transferred to someone who would then hold the gun until it could be then transferred to the final owner when legal age is reached. That's a lot of red tape to give someone your squirrel rifle.

Anti-gun liberals know that more bureaucracy on law-abiding citizens is the easiest form of gun control and hidden under the label of "common sense gun measures." If the government can make criminals out of people that have never committed a criminal act with administrative measures then people will avoid buying, owning and transferring guns altogether. Then they accomplish what they set out to do; stop legal citizens from owning guns.

Guns and Crime

New York City has some of the toughest gun laws in the United States but they have not eliminated crimes committed with guns. Why? Because going after gang members is dangerous, expensive and more often than not the criminal ends up back on the street. Mayors Against Illegal Guns should take a closer look at those that are committing the crimes and focus on punishing the perpetrators rather than building a bureaucracy that is targeted at legal gun owners.

I remember when I was a teenager walking down the street with an Ithaca Model 37 pump 12 gauge in the rural Adirondack mountain town where I grew up. I had purchased the gun from a friend and there wasn't any paperwork, background check, state or federal government involved. A police car pulled up next to me and the officer asked "Are you coming or going? I get off in a few minutes and if you want to go hunting together hop in and I'll give you a ride." It turns out I was walking home and after I told that to the officer, he just said "Ok then, next time" and drove off. To me, that officer exercised common sense gun control. An anti-gun liberal would have had me, the gun seller and probably the officer up on federal charges and locked us up for a long time. It's a pity that the left doesn't understand the relationship between gun ownership and crime but it will be a tragedy if we let the Bloomberg-led coalition erode the gun rights of a free people.

EVALUATING THE AUTHOR'S ARGUMENTS:

In this viewpoint Mike Piccione claims that liberal legislators want to close the "gun show loophole." Based on the argument of Barack Obama, author of the previous viewpoint, do you think Obama would be in favor of closing the loophole? Give specific textual support for your answer.

Facts About Gun Control

Editor's note: These facts can be used in reports or papers to reinforce or add credibility when making important points or claims.

Gun Ownership in America

According to a 2011 Gallup Poll:

- 47 percent of American households have a gun in the home or elsewhere on their property (such as in a garage, barn, shed, or automobile), but only 34 percent of Americans say that they personally own a gun;
- 55 percent of those tending toward the Republican Party reported a gun in the home, whereas only 40 percent of these leaning toward the Democratic Party reported that there was a gun somewhere on their property;
- 46 percent of men said they personally owned a gun, whereas only 23 percent of women said they personally owned a gun;
- 54 percent of American households in the South, 51 percent in the Midwest, 43 percent of those in the West, and 36 percent of American households in the East reported gun ownership.

According to a 2010 Harris poll, among households having a gun:

- 74 percent have a rifle or shotgun;
- 68 percent own a handgun;
- 17 percent have a semiautomatic weapon;
- 8 percent have another type of gun; and
- 2 percent are unsure of the gun type.

Gun Violence in America

According to the Centers for Disease Control and Prevention:

- 73,505 people in America suffered nonfatal injuries as a result of a firearm gunshot in 2010, a rate of 24 per 100,000;
- 25,423 firearm homicides and 34,235 firearm suicides occurred in one year (2006–2007) in America.

- In 2006–2007, Louisiana had the highest firearms death rate in the country, at 20 per 100,000 residents, whereas Hawaii had the lowest, at 3 per 100,000.

Youth Gun Violence

According to the Centers for Disease Control and Prevention:
- 15,135 Americans aged 10 to 19 years suffered nonfatal injuries as a result of a firearm gunshot in 2010, a rate of 35 per 100,000;
- 4,166 firearm homicides and 1,446 firearm suicides among youth aged 10 to 19 years occurred in America in 2006–2007.
- In 2006–2007, the city of New Orleans, Louisiana, had the highest rate of firearm homicides among youth, at 106 per 100,000 residents aged 10 to 19.

Gun Control Laws in America

According to the Legal Community Against Violence:
- Seven states (California, Connecticut, the District of Columbia, Hawaii, Maryland, Massachusetts, New Jersey, and New York) have enacted laws banning assault weapons, while Minnesota, and Virginia regulate assault weapons.
- All states except for Illinois have a process for issuing concealed firearm permits.
- The Brady Handgun Violence Prevention Act requires federally licensed firearms dealers to perform background checks on prospective purchasers, but the act does not apply to unlicensed or private sellers.

According to the Gallup organization:
- 26 percent of Americans in 2011 said there should be a law that would ban the possession of handguns except by the police or other authorized persons, whereas 73 percent said there should not be such a ban.
- Twenty years prior, in 1991, 60 percent of Americans said there should be a law that would ban the possession of handguns except by the police or other authorized persons, whereas 36 percent said there should not be such a ban.

- 43 percent of Americans in 2011 said there should be a law that would make it illegal to manufacture, sell, or possess semiautomatic guns known as assault rifles, whereas 53 percent were against the passage of such a law.
- Twenty years prior, in 1991, 57 percent of Americans said there should be a law that would make it illegal to manufacture, sell, or possess semiautomatic guns known as assault rifles, whereas 42 percent were against the passage of such a law.
- 44 percent of Americans in 2011 said they felt the laws covering the sale of firearms should be kept as they are, 43 percent said the laws should be more strict, and 11 percent said they felt the laws should be less strict.
- Twenty years prior, in 1991, 17 percent of Americans said they felt the laws covering the sale of firearms should be kept as they were, 78 percent said the laws should be more strict, and 2 percent said they felt the laws should be less strict.

A 2008 Gallup poll found that 73 percent of Americans believe the Second Amendment to the US Constitution guarantees the rights of individuals to own guns, whereas 20 percent believe that the Second Amendment only guarantees rights of state militia members to own guns.

Organizations to Contact

The editors have compiled the following list of organizations concerned with the issues debated in this book. The descriptions are derived from materials provided by the organizations. All have publications or information available for interested readers. The list was compiled on the date of publication of the present volume; the information provided here may change. Be aware that many organizations take several weeks or longer to respond to inquiries, so allow as much time as possible for the receipt of requested materials.

Brady Center to Prevent Gun Violence
1225 Eye St. NW, Ste. 1100, Washington, DC 20005
(202) 289-7319 • fax: (202) 408-1851
website: www.bradycenter.org

The Brady Center to Prevent Handgun Violence is a nonprofit, nonpartisan organization working to make it harder for convicted felons, the dangerously mentally ill, and others like them to get guns. Through the Brady Campaign to Prevent Handgun Violence and its network of Million Mom March chapters, the Brady Center rallies for sensible gun laws, regulations, and public policies; and works to educate the public about gun violence. Available at its website are numerous fact sheets, studies, and reports about gun control regulations, gun trafficking, public opinion, and other issues.

Cato Institute
1000 Massachusetts Ave. NW, Washington, DC 20001
(202) 842-0200 • fax: (202) 842-3490
website: www.cato.org

The Cato Institute is a public policy research organization dedicated to the principles of individual liberty, limited government, free markets, and peace. The institute is dedicated to increasing and enhancing the understanding of key public policies and to realistically analyzing their impact on the principles identified above. The Cato Institute publishes many publications, such as the quarterly *Regulation* magazine, the bimonthly *Cato Policy Report*, and the periodic *Cato Journal*.

Coalition to Stop Gun Violence (CSGV)

1424 L St. NW, Ste. 2-1, Washington, DC 20005
(202) 408-0061
e-mail: csgv@csgv.org
website: www.csgv.org

The CSGV is composed of forty-eight national organizations working to reduce gun violence. The coalition seeks to secure freedom from gun violence through research, strategic engagement, and effective policy advocacy. The CSGV publishes many reports, including "America's Gun Shows: Open Markets for Criminals."

Jews for the Preservation of Firearms Ownership (JPFO)

PO Box 270143, Hartford, WI 53027
(262) 673-9745 • fax: (262) 673-9746
e-mail: jpfo@jpfo.org
website: www.jpfo.org

The JPFO a nonprofit organization with the goal of opposing and reversing gun control. The organization works to educate the public on the danger of gun control policies. The JPFO has produced several films on the issue of gun control, including *Innocents Betrayed* and *2A Today for the USA*, and publishes information on its website.

Mayors Against Illegal Guns

909 Third Ave., New York, NY 10022
website: www.mayorsagainstillegalguns.org

Mayors Against Illegal Guns is a coalition of over six hundred mayors from big cities and small towns in America who all share the goal of preventing criminals from illegally obtaining guns. The organization develops and shares strategies for fighting illegal guns. Mayors Against Illegal Guns publishes reports available on its website, including "The Movement of Illegal Guns in America."

National Firearms Association (NFA)

PO Box 52183, Edmonton, AB T6G 2T5, Canada
(877) 818-0393 • fax: (780) 439-4091
website: www.nfa.ca

The NFA is a Canadian organization that works to protect safe and responsible use of firearms. It supports practical gun laws across Canada and provides access to legal assistance for the defense of the gun rights of Canadians. The NFA publishes the *Canadian Firearms Journal.*

National Institute of Justice (NIJ)

810 Seventh St. NW, Washington, DC 20531
(800) 851-3420
website: www.nij.gov

The NIJ is the research, development, and evaluation agency of the US Department of Justice, dedicated to improving knowledge and understanding of crime and justice issues through science. It provides objective and independent information and tools to reduce crime and promote justice, particularly at the state and local levels. The NIJ provides data, graphs, and reports about gun violence, which are available on its website.

National Rifle Association (NRA)

11250 Waples Mill Rd., Fairfax, VA 22030
(703) 267-1000 • fax: (703) 267-3989
website: www.nra.org

The NRA is America's largest organization of gun owners and a powerful pro–gun rights group. The NRA's Institute for Legislative Action lobbies against restrictive gun control legislation. In addition to fact sheets published by the Institute for Legislative Action are the journals *American Rifleman, American Hunter,* and *America's 1st Freedom.*

Second Amendment Committee

PO Box 1776, Hanford, CA 93232
(559) 584-5209 • fax: (559) 584-4084
e-mail: liberty89@libertygunrights.com
website: www.libertygunrights.com

The Second Amendment Committee, founded by a longtime gun-rights activist, is a nationwide organization that aims to protect the right to keep and bear arms. The committee has authored pro-gun legislation and has a variety of documents available on its website.

Second Amendment Foundation (SAF)
12500 NE Tenth Pl., Bellevue, WA 98005
(800) 426-4302 • fax: (425) 451-3959
e-mail: adminforweb@saf.org
website: www.saf.org

The SAF is dedicated to promoting a better understanding of the constitutional heritage to privately own and possess firearms. The foundation develops educational and legal action programs designed to better inform the public about the gun control debate. The SAF publishes *Gun Week*, the *Journal on Firearms & Public Policy, Women & Guns*, and the *Gottlieb-Tartaro Report*.

Stop Handgun Violence (SHV)
One Bridge St., Ste. 300, Newton, MA 02458
(877) SAFE ARMS (723-3276) • fax: (617) 965-7308
e-mail: shv@stophandgunviolence.com
website: www.stophandgunviolence.com

The SHV is a nonprofit organization committed to the prevention of gun violence through public awareness and legislation, without banning guns. It aims to increase public awareness about gun violence through media and public education campaigns. Available on its website are gun violence facts, stories, and information about its media campaigns.

Violence Policy Center (VPC)
1730 Rhode Island Ave. NW, Ste. 1014, Washington, DC 20036
(202) 822-8200
website: www.vpc.org

The VPC is a nonprofit organization that aims to stop death and injury from firearms. The center conducts research on gun violence in America and works to develop violence-reduction policies and proposals. The VPC publishes studies on a range of gun-violence issues, including "States with Higher Gun Ownership and Weak Gun Laws Lead Nation in Gun Death."

For Further Reading

Books

Burbick, Joan. *Gun Show Nation: Gun Culture and American Democracy.* New York: New Press, 2007. Examines the politics of gun ownership and explores a conservative ideology that the author claims attempts to place gun ownership at the center of American democracy.

Canada, Geoffrey. *Fist, Stick, Knife, Gun: A Personal History of Violence.* Boston: Beacon, 2010. Recounts a childhood in the South Bronx where violence was part of growing up, starting with fist fighting and culminating in gun violence.

Cornell, Saul. *A Well-Regulated Militia: The Founding Fathers and the Origins of Gun Control in America.* New York: Oxford University Press, 2008. Argues that the founders understood the right to bear arms as neither an individual nor a collective right, but as a civic right.

Cramer, Clayton E. *Armed America: The Remarkable Story of How and Why Guns Became as American as Apple Pie.* Nashville: Nelson Current, 2009. Traces the winding historical trail of United States citizens' passion for firearms, arguing that Americans have always been dependent on firearms.

Doherty, Brian. *Gun Control on Trial: Inside the Supreme Court Battle over the Second Amendment.* Washington, DC: Cato Institute, 2008. Tells story behind the landmark *District of Columbia v. Heller* (2008) ruling, providing a look at the inside stories of the case.

Goss, Kristin A. *Disarmed: The Missing Movement for Gun Control in America.* Princeton, NJ: Princeton University Press, 2008. Suggests that the gun control campaign has been stymied by a combination of factors, analyzing the dilemmas faced by advocates of gun control.

Gottlieb, Alan, and Dave Workman. *Shooting Blanks: Facts Don't Matter to the Gun Ban Crowd.* Bellevue, WA: Merril, 2011. Explores the issues underlying the continuing battle for the right to keep and bear arms, arguing in favor of gun rights.

Harcourt, Bernard E. *Language of the Gun: Youth, Crime, and Public Policy*. Chicago: University of Chicago Press, 2006. Recounts in-depth interviews with incarcerated youths about the meaning of guns, claiming that their answers reveal assumptions implicit in current handgun policies.

Hemenway, David. *Private Guns, Public Health*. Ann Arbor: University of Michigan Press, 2006. Argues that there are advantages in treating gun violence as a consumer safety and public health problem rather than as a natural consequence of America's high rates of violence.

Lott, John R., Jr. *More Guns, Less Crime: Understanding Crime and Gun-Control Laws*. 3rd ed. Chicago: University of Chicago Press, 2010. Challenges common perceptions about the relationship of guns, crime, and violence, including analysis of the effects of gun bans in Chicago and Washington, DC.

Melzer, Scott. *Gun Crusaders: The NRA's Culture War*. New York: New York University Press, 2009. Claims that the National Rifle Association constructs and perceives threats to gun rights as one more attack in a broad cultural war.

Norquist, Grover Glenn. *Leave Us Alone: Getting the Government's Hands Off Our Money, Our Guns, Our Lives*. New York: HarperCollins, 2009. Argues that there are two competing coalitions in American politics, with the Republican Party now controlled largely by a movement wanting the government to leave people alone.

Souter, Gerry. *American Shooter: A Personal History of Gun Culture in the United States*. Washington, DC: Potomac, 2012. Provides a unique look at gun ownership, handgun bans, shooting sports, and the controversy over how to interpret the Second Amendment from the point of view of a politically liberal gun owner and enthusiast.

Taylor, Jimmy D. *American Gun Culture: Collectors, Shows, and the Story of the Gun*. El Paso, TX: LFB, 2009. Explores the symbolic meaning of guns and the ways in which the meaning assigned to guns influences gun ownership and use.

Tushnet, Mark V. *Out of Range: Why the Constitution Can't End the Battle over Guns.* New York: Oxford University Press, 2007. Offers a guide to both sides of the argument over gun rights in America, offering solutions that could calm, if not settle, the bitter dispute.

Wilson, Harry L. *Guns, Gun Control, and Elections: The Politics and Policy of Firearms.* Lanham, MD: Rowman & Littlefield, 2006. Examines current gun control policy and explains how it was adopted by discussing the roles and interactions of elected officials, interest groups, political parties, and the public.

Winkler, Adam. *Gunfight: The Battle over the Right to Bear Arms in America.* New York: Norton, 2011. Argues that guns—rather than abortion, race, or religion—are at the heart of America's cultural divide.

Periodicals and Internet Sources

Barnett, Randy. "The Supreme Court's Gun Showdown," *Wall Street Journal*, June 29, 2010.

Bell, Larry. "UN Agreement Should Have All Gun Owners Up in Arms," *Forbes*, June 7, 2011. www.forbes.com.

Bernstein, David E. "Liberals, Conservatives, and Individual Rights," Cato Institute, June 27, 2008. www.cato.org.

Blackman, Josh, and Ilya Shapiro. "Supreme Court Opens Door to More Liberty," *Detroit (MI) News*, July 5, 2010.

Cannon, Michael F. "Still Limits on Second Amendment," *Orange County (CA) Register*, July 1, 2008.

Carpenter, Ted Galen. "Are Lax US Gun Laws Fueling Mexico's Drug Violence?," *National Interest*, March 11, 2011.

Chapman, Steve. "The Unconcealed Truth About Carrying Guns: What the Gun Control Lobby Doesn't Want You to Know," *Reason*, March 31, 2011.

Doherty, Brian. "Gun Control Couldn't Have Stopped It," *Reason*, April 2011.

Falconer, Bruce. "Semiautomatic for the People," *Mother Jones*, July/ August 2008.

Feldman, Clarice, and Rosslyn Smith. "The Changing Face of Gun Ownership," *American Thinker*, August 3, 2010. www.american thinker.com.

Florida, Richard. "The Geography of Gun Deaths," *Atlantic*, January 13, 2011.

Fricke, John. "Should I Buy a Gun?," *American Thinker*, November 17, 2011. www.americanthinker.com.

Good, Chris. "The Supreme Court Ruling and Gun Politics," *Atlantic*, June 28, 2010.

Heiser, James. "Concealed Carry Soon to Be Legal in Wisconsin," *New American*, June 28, 2011.

Heuvel, Katrina vanden. "Gun (In)Sanity," *Nation*, June 2, 2009.

Johnson, Richard L. "Protect the Second Amendment: Teach a Child to Shoot," *Human Events*, September 28, 2011.

Jonsson, Patrik. "More Guns Equal More Crime? Not in 2009, FBI Crime Report Shows," *Christian Science Monitor*, December 23, 2009.

Kaminsky, Ross. "The Second Amendment, Incorporated," *American Spectator*, June 29, 2010.

Kanazawa, Satoshi. "The Second Amendment Right to Keep and Bear Nuclear Weapons: The Second Amendment Has Nothing Specifically to Do with Guns," *Psychology Today*, February 20, 2011.

Klarevas, Louis. "Closing the Gap: How to Reform US Gun Laws to Prevent Another Tucson," *New Republic*, January 13, 2011.

Kopel, David. "Gun Rights and the Constitution: Was *Heller* Insignificant?," *New Ledger*, March 26, 2009. www.newledger.com.

Kumeh, Titania. "Do Guns and College Mix?," *Mother Jones*, September 30, 2010. www.motherjones.com.

Lazare, Daniel. "Arms and the Right," *Nation*, May 5, 2008.

Levy, Robert A. "Gun Control Measures Don't Stop Violence," CNN, January 19, 2011. www.cnn.com.

Lopez, Kathryn Jean. "Rounding Up the Guns," *National Review Online*, January 13, 2011. www.nationalreview.com.

Los Angeles Times, "Guns and States' Rights," November 18, 2011.

Lott, John. "Gun-Show Bill Would Do More Harm than Good," Newsmax, February 2, 2011. www.newsmax.com.

May, Clifford D. "Thank You for Not Packing Heat," *National Review Online*, January 11, 2011. www.nationalreview.com.

Mayors Against Illegal Guns. "Trace the Guns: The Link Between Gun Laws and Interstate Gun Trafficking," September 2010. www.mayorsagainstillegalguns.org.

McCormack, John. "We're All Gun Nuts Now: The Democrats Sidle Up to the Second Amendment," *Weekly Standard*, May 19, 2008.

Mencimer, Stephanie. "Whitewashing the Second Amendment," *Mother Jones*, March 19, 2008.

Miron, Jeffrey A. "Strict Gun Control Will Seem like War on Drugs," *Bloomberg Businessweek*, January 13, 2011.

Moran, James. "Moran's News Commentary: 'National Right-to-Carry' Act Is Irresponsible," *Falls Church (VA) News-Press*, November 16, 2011.

Nutter, Michael A., and Charles H. Ramsey. "Don't Ease Gun Permit Rules," *Philadelphia Inquirer*, December 4, 2011.

Paulin, David. "Second Amendment Culture Wars: Eastern Elites vs. Gun-Friendly Red States," *American Thinker*, March 13, 2011. www.americanthinker.com.

Peterson, Dan. "A Splendid, Precarious Victory," *American Spectator*, September 2010.

Piccione, Mike. "Back Door Gun Control and Fighting Back," *Human Events*, June 14, 2011.

Posner, Richard A. "In Defense of Looseness: The Supreme Court and Gun Control," *New Republic*, August 27, 2008.

Rittgers, David. "Be a Good Victim," *National Review Online*, October 22, 2009. www.nationalreview.com.

Sackett, Gary C. "Common Sense Weapons Bill That Would Make Us Safer," *Salt Lake Tribune*, May 27, 2011.

Saletan, William. "Friendly Firearms," *Slate*, January 11, 2011. www.slate.com.

Serwer, Adam. "A Gun Rights Case Liberals Wanted to Lose, Just Not like This," *American Prospect*, June 28, 2010.

Shapiro, Ilya, and Josh Blackman. "Using Guns to Protect Liberty," *Washington Times*, February 23, 2010.

Stossel, John. "Guns Save Lives," Creators, June 23, 2010. www.creators.com.

Sullum, Jacob. "Gun Shy: Four Supreme Court Justices Make the Case Against Constitutional Rights," *Reason*, June 30, 2010.

Thomson, Doug. "Another Gun Law Would Not Have Saved Those in Tucson," Capitol Hill Blue, January 12, 2011. www.capitolhill blue.com.

USA Today. "Our View on Guns: Porous Laws Help Lunatics Get Their Hands on Deadly Weapons," January 11, 2011.

Winkler, Adam. "The Secret History of Guns," *Atlantic*, September 2011.

Wittes, Benjamin. "Gun Shy: Let's Stop Interpreting the Second Amendment and Just Abolish It," *New Republic*, March 19, 2007.

Websites

Bureau of Justice Statistics (bjs.ojp.usdoj.gov). This website of the US Office of Justice Programs offers firearms and crime statistics for the United States.

Legal Community Against Violence (www.lcav.org). This website of a public interest law center is dedicated to preventing gun violence and provides statistics, laws, and publications related to guns and gun violence.

OpenCarry.org (www.opencarry.org). This pro-gun Internet community promotes the right to openly carry a gun and keeps track of gun-carry laws and proposed legislation.

Index

Picture Credits

© AP Images, 105

© AP Images/Elise Amendola, 37

© AP Images/Victoria Arocho, 53

© AP Images/Judi Bottoni, 108

© AP Images/Harry Cabluck, 84

© AP Images/Chicago Sun-Times, Rich Hein, 21

© AP Images/Dennis Cook, 55

© AP Images/Pablo Martinez Monsivais, 15, 93

© AP Images/Douglas C. Pizac, 79

© AP Images/Mark Stehle, 88

© Terry Ashe/Time & Life Pictures/Getty Images, 74

© Jon-Are Berg-Jacobsen/AFP/Getty Images, 99

© Lili DeBarbieri/AFP/Getty Images, 50

Gale/Cengage Learning, 16, 22, 29, 34, 41, 57, 63, 69, 73, 80, 86, 97, 103,

© Alexis C. Glenn/UPI/Landov, 67

© Chuck Kennedy/MCT/MCT via Getty images, 26

© Reuters/Landov, 61

© Jim West/Alamy, 11, 44